Bible Study Guide & Workbook

Jeanette Wills

I have learned over the years that it is not on the mountaintops where people find themselves drawn to God ... but in the valleys.

Jeanette Wills

Contents

Forward

We are living in very uncertain times. Fear and anxiety abound. Many people are still processing the sudden death of loved ones during Covid 19, while others are trying to make sense of our war-ridden world. Still, others are burdened with the failing economy and fear for their future and their children's future.

As you embark on this journey through this Bible Study Guide and Workbook, your encounter with God will bring healing, a better understanding of the Bible, and a closer relationship with God, leading to an unexplainable peace.

6Do not be anxious about anything, but in every situation, by prayer and petition, with thanksgiving, present your requests to God.
7And the peace of God, which transcends all understanding, will guard your hearts and your minds in Christ Jesus.

Philippians 4: 6-7 (NKJV)

He who holds the future also holds your hand!

Introduction

Welcome to this Bible Study Guide and Workbook! This study guide has been designed for you to experience God in various ways. The best way to get the most out of these lessons is to complete each day as it is laid out. Each day offers scripture-backed insight and wisdom followed by a daily promise, personal questions, a prayer pertaining to the lesson, and space to journal.

Take the time to ponder the lessons and scriptures, allowing the Lord to speak to you. Internalize what the promise following the lesson is saying to you. Think about how the promise can impact your life.

As you answer the questions, following the promise, be still, if necessary, wait for the Holy Spirit to bring answers to your mind.

Each day's prayer is designed to bring you closer to God through sincere communication, so continue dialoguing with God should you feel led to do so. He loves to hear from you!

Following the prayer is space to journal. What you write here could be your thoughts about any gained insight, something God specifically spoke to you about, or even a request you may have. Journaling can be anything you want to write pertaining to the lesson.

Finally, the book offers group study questions. This Bible Study Guide and Workbook provides an excellent opportunity to study as a group. As a once-a-week bible study, you and your group may opt to do one day per week or cover several lessons per week. What an excellent opportunity to grow together with others as you share one another's experiences.

Day 1 - *God Gets You!*

Have you ever felt like an island…, alone in the middle of nowhere? People can be all around you, and yet you still feel isolated. Maybe you know many people but are known by few. Many people have a sense of not being understood by anyone. Even Christians can experience this if they don't know, have forgotten, or perhaps lost sight of God's intentional mindfulness of us.

Let's take a look at what God has to say about you.

Jeremiah 1:5 (NIV)
"Before I formed you in the womb, I knew you, before you were born, I set you apart;

First of all, God says *He* formed you in the womb. You were a plan before you were born. He knew every aspect of who you are and will be. You are not and were not an afterthought, a mistake, or even someone else's plan. You are here because God had you in mind and knows you well.

He understands how you think. He understands how you feel. He knows what you're going to say before you say it. He knows how you're going to process your life experiences. He knows just how much pressure you can take. He even knows the weaknesses of your physical body. He knows your propensities - both good and evil. He knows your hidden thoughts and what brings you joy and sorrow. He knows when you will have victory and when you will fail. He knows what you fully understand and what you do not. He knows the limitations of your mind and body. He knows your heart, your desires, and your true intentions. Here's the good news…He knows you and loves you!

1

David, amid a very difficult period of his life, wrote the following:

Psalm 139:1-18 (NIV)
¹ You have searched me, Lord, and you know me.

There is nothing about you that is hidden from God. Not only are your hidden thoughts or desires laid bare before Him, but even down to the slightest nonnormality in your body.

² You know when I sit and when I rise; you perceive Thoughts from afar.

The Lord knows whether you are resting or getting up in the morning. He knows what you are thinking and will be thinking before you have even begun to consider it. It only makes sense to be perfectly honest when talking to God. What could be the benefit of praying insincerely, knowing He knows your thoughts and heart? We are transparent before Him. Though, often, I don't believe people are fully aware of what's in their own heart.

Here's an example: I have had people tell me over the years that they pray to God that if He would allow them to win the lottery, they would bless other people with their winnings. So often, these have been the least generous people I have ever met. Selfishness, greed, and lust for money is how they have lived their life. Sometimes, I can't help but wonder if they have entirely deceived themselves or if they think they are tricking God. The knowledge that God knows even our hidden motives should be sobering, leading us to sincere communication with God.

³ You discern my going out and my lying down; you are familiar with all my ways.

Your activities throughout the day, even what you lay in bed pondering, are known by God.

⁴ Before a word is on my tongue you, Lord, know it completely.

Before your tongue can form your thoughts, God already knows what you will say.

⁵ You hem me in behind and before, and you lay your hand upon me.

He has you surrounded and protected.

⁶ Such knowledge is too wonderful for me, too lofty for me to attain.

God's knowledge is so amazing and entirely beyond our scope of understanding.

⁷ Where can I go from your Spirit? Where can I flee from your presence?

Have you ever felt like you breached a line or went too far? So far, even repentance won't redeem you? A place where God will no longer hear you, answer, or see you? Here's the great news! That place does not exist! The adversary would love to convince you otherwise, but as usual, he's doing what he does best...lying! There is no place you can find yourself out of God's reach, His grace, mercy, and forgiveness.

⁸ If I go up to the heavens, you are there; if I make my bed in the depths, you are there.

It is wonderful to know that even when you make choices that land you in a terrible situation, God does not leave you. We may not be rescued from the circumstance or be exempt from consequences, but know that God is still with us through it.

> [9] *If I rise on the wings of the dawn, if I settle on the far side of the sea,*
> [10] *even there, your hand will guide me, your right hand will hold me fast.*

God is not only with you in places that seem remote, but His authority in your life stands. He holds the bottom line... the final say-so. There is no entity on earth that can override God's authority.

What may seem unchartered territory for you is not for Him. He knows what you don't know and will guide you.

> [11] *If I say, "Surely the darkness will hide me and the light becomes night around me,"*
> [12] *even the darkness will not be dark to you; the night will shine like the day, for darkness is as light to you.*

Can you fathom a God that is so light that the darkest moments in your life, times when there seems to be no path to escape, no recourse that doesn't lead to disaster, yet for God, your situation is not hidden, and He already has the answer?

> [13] *For you created my inmost being; you knit me together in my mother's womb.*

14 I praise you because I am fearfully and wonderfully made; your works are wonderful, I know that full well.
15 My frame was not hidden from you when I was made in the secret place, when I was woven together in the depths of the earth.
16 Your eyes saw my unformed body; all the days ordained for me were written in your book before one of them came to be.
17 How precious to me are your thoughts, oh God! How vast is the sum of them!
18 Were I to count them, they would outnumber the grains of sand — when I awake, I am still with you.

David wrote Psalm 139 while King Saul was relentlessly pursuing him. It brought David much comfort to know that God was right there with him anywhere he found himself. When the knowledge of God's continuous presence with us becomes a permanent part of our consciousness, our fears and anxiety will diminish and be replaced with a deep sense of gratitude and hope.

Today's Promise

Call to Me, and I will answer you and show you great and mighty things which you did not know.

Jeremiah 33:3

Questions

David was exiled from his people for eight years and pursued by Saul. During these tumultuous years of young

David's life, what can we learn from David's response to a long-lasting trial?

_____

_____

_____

_____

_____

What part of Psalm 139 mainly speaks to you?

_____

_____

_____

_____

_____

Today's Prayer

Dear Lord, thank you for your never-failing love and attentiveness to me. I praise You!

For you fearfully and wonderfully made me! I am grateful to know I am never beyond Your reach. Please allow me to remember I am never alone; let me feel your presence when I feel lonely and misunderstood. Please help me to remember you are always with me and know me even better than I know myself.

6

Thoughts

_____

_____

_____

_____

_____

Group Study Questions

Share what difficulties you have faced and how you responded or are responding.

The Bible tells us that David had several hundred men who supported him. Do you think it was possible for him to feel still alone?

What about Psalm 139 gives the impression that David knew God intimately?

What about Psalm 139 can change your focus in difficult times?

Day 2 - *The Treasure Hunt Begins*

Isaiah 55:6 (NIV)
Seek the Lord while He can be found; call on Him
while He is near.

1 Chronicles 16:11 (NIV)
Seek out the Lord and His Strength; seek His face
always.

Welcome to Day 2! You now know or are reminded of how well God knows you from Day 1's lesson. Now the question is, how well do you know God? I am excited that you have chosen to seek the Lord to establish a closer relationship with Him.

All too often, relationships fade because we neglect to invest in them. Once we have a general knowledge of a person, we often stop learning them. Husbands and wives frequently surprise one another by seemingly acting out of character when that may be who that person has always been. The spouse often overlooks signs of the person's character, or perhaps the person has been metamorphosizing right in front of their spouse…again…unnoticed by the spouse. For many people, once they believe they have gathered the information about someone that meets their needs, the interest level in learning more about them often declines.

Whether you have children or remember being one, children can be another example of our failure to invest continuously and consistently. Parents can see familiar traits or tendencies in their children and forget that they are forever changing as they grow with many influences that the parents are unaware of.

8

On the other hand, children may learn the predictable behavior of their parents and assume that is all there is to their parents, able to predict their parent's response but never understanding the '*Why*'.

Parents and children often think they know each other well when they may not. A relationship takes a consistent effort from both parties since people are forever changing - being exposed and shaped by new experiences. Overestimating your knowledge of someone can lead to a significant loss by limiting the relationship's potential. It can also lead to deep disappointment when traits come to the surface that can no longer be ignored.

We must be attentive to relationships that truly matter to us. If you want a close and meaningful relationship with someone, then learning all you can about them is imperative. By the way, I might add... that door swings both ways. It is also essential to be honest and transparent if a genuine relationship is to be gained. I am bringing up human relationships because how we treat God is not so different from how we treat one another. The people we invest in are the people we know best. That often requires time spent with that person. The same applies to our relationship with God. How valuable are the words sent in a card saying 'I love you, appreciate you, and value our relationship' yet never a phone call or visit? Listening and talking with a person on a phone call or even sitting with the person ...even if minimal words transpire... the message 'you are valued, loved or appreciated' is received and believed.

Unlike ever-changing people, God is consistent. He is the same *Yesterday, Today, and Forever,* and yet, it still takes purposed effort to have a robust and meaningful relationship with God, not because He changes but because there is so much about Him that can only be learned from Him, which, requires spending time with Him. The Lord reveals more about who He is the closer you draw to Him.

To proceed in our effort to seek God's face, we first must understand God's holiness.

Holy is the most used term in the Bible to describe God. It is the only term in the Bible repeated three times in a row...twice!

Revelation 4:6-8 (NIV)

6 In the center, around the throne, were four living creatures, and they were covered with ice, in front and in the back.

7 The first living creature was like a lion, the second was like an ox, the third had the face of a man, the fourth was like a flying eagle.

8 Each of the four living creatures had six wings, and was covered with ice all and even under its wings. Day and night, they never stop saying "Holy, holy, holy is the Lord God, Almighty, who was, and is, and is to come."

Isaiah 6:1-3 (NIV)

1 In the year that King Uzziah died, I saw the Lord, high and exalted, seated on the throne; and the train of His robe filled the temple.

2 Above Him were seraphim, each with six wings: With two wings they covered their faces; with two they covered their feet, and with two they were flying.

3 And they were calling to one another: "Holy, holy, holy is the Lord Almighty. The whole earth is full of His Glory."

The mere fact that Holy is repeated three times is significant. A word mentioned in succession in the Bible three times indicates the point is being emphasized and elevated to the third degree, unmatched or superlative. God's holiness cannot be measured; it is infinite.

Isaiah, the prophet, refers to God as "The Holy One" thirty times in the Book of Isaiah.

Though Holy is often used to describe God's character, it is not just His character; instead, it is *Who He Is*. It is the very essence of His being. Divine and Holy are, in this sense of the word, synonymous.

God's profound holiness separates Him from all things human, earthly, or created. God was not created; He existed but was never created! God is infinitely exalted above His creation. Holy, in this sense of the term, is not a distinct attribute of God but is a description of all that God is and does. It is the very essence of His being.

Let's look at it this way...because God is holy and morally pure in every way, He is, therefore, righteous (ethically perfect). He is incapable of being unjust. It is impossible for Him to sin. His holiness separates Him from sin. He is incorruptible eternally. He cannot decay or age; he cannot die. His Holiness cannot be penetrated just as darkness cannot penetrate light. He is light.

1 John 1:5
This is the message we have heard from Him and declare to you: God is light; in him, there is no darkness at all.

There is no other side to God. All light... no darkness in any part of His being.

Humans became sinful, corrupt beings through their disobedience in the garden. This account can be found in Genesis chapters 2 and 3. Holiness is so powerful a light force that corrupt man in his natural state could not withstand the presence of the incorruptible God. Without a provision provided by God, anyone or something less than perfect that comes in contact with such holiness would be destroyed. To enter into His presence, we must be sanctified – made clean or pure through the blood of Jesus, repentance and faith in Jesus as the Son of God, and His death and resurrection.

Today's Promise

Ask, and it will be given to you; seek, and you will find, knock and it will be opened to you. For everyone who asks, receives, and he who seeks finds, and to him who knocks it will be opened.

Matthew 7:7-8

Questions

What can you do to seek God's face? What does seeking God's face look like?

_____

_____

_____

_____

_____

Have you ever over or underestimated someone in your life? If so, what were the consequences or benefits?

_____

_____

_____

_____

_____

What impact does God's holiness have on your life?

_____

_____

_____

_____

_____

What stands out to you about God's holiness

_____

_____

_____

_____

_____

Thoughts

_____

_____

13

_____

_____

_____

Today's Prayer

Lord, I am so grateful that You care so much for me and are attentive to every aspect of my life. Lord, as I learn to seek Your face, let the things I know about you take root. Forgive me for not always cherishing our relationship as the precious gift that it is. Help me to be mindful of You in all of my doings. Fill me with your Holy Spirit so He can lead me and bring all things to my memory that I am learning about you. Give me the strength to pursue a relationship with You with all my heart, to seek You relentlessly as I would a treasure.

Group Study Questions

Have each person share their favorite attribute of God.

What stands in your way from seeking God?

How well do you feel you know God?

How would you describe your relationship with God?

How would you rate a relationship if you only hear from the person when they need something from you?

Can we be holy?

14

Day 3 - *The Top of the Ladder*

Welcome to Day 3. When someone takes the time to get to know who you are, it makes you feel valued, appreciated and loved. God is no different. Learning who God is is one way we *"draw near to God, and He will draw near to you." James 4:8.*

For the next few days, we will explore who God says He is and His attributes. In all we learn about the Father, keep in mind the following four verses:

John 1:1-3 (NKJV)
¹ In the beginning was the Word, and the Word was with God: and the Word was God.
² The same was in the beginning with God.
³ All things were made by Him and without Him there was nothing made that was made

.

John 1:14 (NKJV)
And the Word became flesh and dwelt among us, and we beheld His glory, the glory, as of the only begotten, son, of the Father, full of grace and truth.

The Son of God, Jesus, also called The Word - as we learn in verse 14 - was in the beginning with God. Though they are separate beings, they are one. The third entity is the Holy Spirit. The Holy Spirit of God the father is God also. God the Father, God the Son, and God the Holy Spirit are how we conclude that God is three distinct people in one nature, three equal co-eternal persons sharing the same essence.

As you embark on getting to know God in a more profound sense today, you will explore His omnipotence.

Omnipotence means 'All-Powerful.' Some of you might think. 'Got it... enough said'. I want to challenge you to take a deeper look and consider the magnitude of omnipotence.

Job 11:7-11 (NIV)

[7] *"Can you fathom the mysteries of God? Can you probe the limits of the Almighty?*
[8] *They are higher than the heavens ---what can you do? They are deeper than the depths of the grave---what can you know?*
[9] *Their measure is longer than the Earth and wider than the sea.*
[10] *If he comes along and can find you in a prison and confines convenes, a court, who can oppose him?*
[11] *Surely he recognizes deceitful men, and when he sees evil, does he not take note?*

You and I are incapable of comprehending the vastness of His wonderous ways. We can never know enough about God, but the more we seek Him, the more of Him He reveals to us.

Some of you taking this journey may feel you already know God well, while others may be just getting to know the Lord. In both cases, reflecting on what you learn through this study or being reminded of what you already know about His attributes will strengthen your relationship with Him.

Isaiah 43:13 (NIV)

Yes, and from the ancient days, I am He. No one can deliver out of my hand. When I act, who can reverse it?

16

There was no one before His existence. God existed before there was a day, a night, or Earth. If a person relies on false gods to help them, if they have kindled God's wrath against them, they are doomed! No power in the heavens or on earth can deliver one from God's judgment.

Read what He says about those who follow Him.

John 10: 27-30 (NIV)
[27] My sheep listen to my voice; I know them, and they follow me.
[28] I give them eternal life, and they shall never perish; no one can snatch them out of my hand.
[29] My Father, who has given them to me, is greater than all; no one can snatch them out of my Father's hand.
[30] I and the father are one.

The same hand of God mentioned in verse 29 is the same hand that holds you; no one can take you out of His hand! Take a moment to digest this reality. You are in the hands of God! A God that Loves and cares for YOU! He is such a mighty God that no force in the heavens, the earth, or below can separate us from His Love!

Your everyday existence is in His hands alone. Whatever God decides to do, no one or anything can stop Him. Nor can anyone or anything reverse what He has decided to do. All Mighty! Omnipotent! God has complete and total control of *EVERYTHING*! His words are so powerful that He spoke this world into existence.

Psalm 33:6 (NIV)
By the word of the Lord were the heavens made, their starry host by the breath of His mouth.

Psalm 115:3 (NIV)
Our God is in the heavens; He does all that He pleases.

Jeremiah 32:17 (NIV)
Ah, Sovereign Lord, you have made the heavens and the Earth by your great power and outstretched arm. Nothing is too hard for you.

Matthew 19:26 (NIV)
Jesus looked at them and said, "With man, this is impossible, but with God, all things are possible".

It is a wonder that a Being so powerful would create us finite, fragile beings and offer us eternity with Him. Talk about having friends of influence... having God as your friend is as high up the ladder as you can get! Think about what it means to have God, the most powerful Being in existence, as a friend.

When I was about five years old, I had a life-changing experience. We lived in Brooklyn, New York, in a brownstone house. At that time, I had an older brother - 9 years old, and a sister, six years old. We were often sent to the basement to play and were not allowed to come back up to the main floor until called. This particular day, we looked up out the narrow window that revealed the backyard and saw the first snow of the season falling. My older brother asked my sister to go upstairs and ask my mother if we could go outside and play in the snow.

"No. I don't want to get in trouble." my sister replied.

He then asked me if I would go. I agreed to go but under one condition – that the two of them prayed with me first. After joining hands and a simple prayer, I began my hike up the paper-covered basement stairs. My mother was washing dishes as she turned with a cross face to see me standing at her side. I asked, "Can we go outside and play in the snow?"

My mother turned sharply back to the dishes and snapped, "Put on your coat and gloves." I quickly ran down the basement stairs and spread the news.

After playing in the snow, my mother called us to come into the house. It was nearing dinner time. My brother dashed past my mother with my sister close behind. I, too, tried to run past her but she stood before me and said "You, stop!". I froze. She looked more cross than earlier. Looking sharply down at me as I looked up, afraid of what may be coming, she asked, "What did you pull down in the basement?" I just stood there, not completely understanding the question. She continued, "I opened my mouth to say 'no,' and out came 'yes!' Were you down there praying?" She was clearly not happy about this.

I was gripped with fear and barely able to answer "yes." She turned from me, waved her hand in dismissal, and said, "Go on...get out of here!"

That day changed me forever. I realized that God was stronger than Mommy! He was all-powerful! In my small world, no one was more powerful than my mother. Maybe my dad was stronger, but he was at work during the day, so she had all the power over us. From that day forth, I knew that God would hear me, answer me, and protect me. He could make her say things she didn't intend to say! He really does answer prayer! He is the *Top of the Ladder*!

Know this. God is more powerful than any supervisor, manager, or authoritative figure in your life. God is the ultimate authority in your life. As His child, you can go directly to Him, who has the final say on everything. God is the CEO and owner of heaven, earth, and everything else! He can remove unjust people from positions and change minds and hearts.

Isaiah 41: 10 (NIV)
So do not fear, for I am with you; do not be dismayed, for I am your God. I will strengthen you and help you; I will uphold you with my righteous right hand.

What better hand to be held by? The Most High God, the Omnipotent God of All, is willing to strengthen *you*, help *you,* and keep *you*! How fortunate we are to know an *All-powerful God!*

Whatever trial you may be facing today, know without a doubt that God has *you* in His hands. He did not let go of you. He has not forgotten about you. His Love for you has not wavered. He will see you through whatever you are facing. Your testimony is being built.

Today's Promise

28 *The Lord is the everlasting God, the Creator of the ends of the earth. He does not faint or grow weary; his understanding is unsearchable.*
29 *He gives power to the faint, and to him who has no might increases strength.*

Isaiah 40:28-29

Questions

How is God's omnipotence demonstrated in John 10:27-30?

_____

_____

_____

_____

_____

What promises are found in John 10:27-30?

_____

_____

_____

_____

Is God's omnipotence beneficial to you? If so…how?

_____

_____

_____

_____

Is there an answered prayer that was a defining moment for you? Is there an experience that was pivotal in establishing your faith?

_____

_____

_____

_____

Today's Prayer

Our Father in Heaven, Lord Jesus, is seated at the Father's right hand. I am so humbled as I ponder the greatness of Your power! I am so grateful that you hold my hand. Knowing that someone as powerful as you is with me comforts me. When I am anxious and fearful, bring these scriptures to mind so I can stand on Your Word and have peace.

Thoughts

_____

_____

_____

_____

Group Study Questions

Each person gives examples of God's Omnipotence.

How does this knowledge of God's power affect your life? Thoughts?

How was this power demonstrated in Jesus?

Day 4 - *The Ultimate 'KNOW IT ALL'*

Life on earth is often unpredictable. We have yet to determine what tomorrow holds and what unexpected circumstances may be around the next bend. For some, navigating their current conditions is so challenging they cannot even consider what's next.

Let's look at Covid 19 as an example. Who among the average population saw that coming? Not too many. Covid took most of the world by surprise. Nearly all people around the globe were impacted in one way or another. Many people lost their jobs, life savings, and their businesses were destroyed - not to mention the horrific loss of life.

Families and friends, many already at odds politically, were now facing another dividing force... those getting the vaccine vs. those refusing the vaccine. Mis-information abounded. Most people didn't know what to believe. The elected officials who vowed to have the public's best interest as a top priority could no longer be trusted as their inability to agree on anything amongst themselves cast doubt on everything the public was being told.

The news stations were also at war with each other, making it impossible to know who was telling the truth about any given subject. For many, grave uncertainty is a breeding ground for fear and anxiety. This is the state many people found themselves in, and many are still wrestling with it.

Let me say this... none of what happens is a surprise to God! He is not caught off guard and scratching His head. You did not just happen to be here on earth; right where you are now. God knew what you would be currently facing before you were born. He has already decided how He will use the circumstances for your betterment and His glory. He knows what you will need before you know there will be a need. No matter how uncertain the times, we serve a very capable God. Remember, this All-Knowing GOD LOVES YOU!

We may not know what tomorrow holds...but we know who holds tomorrow! Do you comprehend how liberating it is from fear and uncertainty knowing this provides? Ponder this for just a few moments. Understand that God is in complete control and is aware of everything. Nothing *'slips by'* an All-Knowing God un-noticed. Grasp this realization ...let this seep into your soul. Peace will begin to follow as fear will have to vacate.

Today, we will take our finite minds as far as we can fathom to understand an all-knowing God. Just the thought of so much information about *everything* is unimaginable. Let's see what the Bible can tell us about the omniscient (All-knowing) God.

Psalm 147:5 (NASB)
Great is our Lord and abundant in strength; His understanding is infinite.

There is no ending to God's understanding. He understands you far beyond your ability to understand yourself.

Matthew 10:30 (KJV)
But the very hairs of your head are all numbered.

This omniscient God already knows how many hairs are on your head! Could a God who is mindful of the number of hairs on your head be unaware or insensitive to your needs, fears, and concerns? Absolutely not! He is aware when one sparrow falls from the sky. You are so much more valuable to Him than a sparrow. The Lord calls us His children. He has paid a great price so we would not perish. Therefore, doesn't it stand to reason that He knows all your concerns and would never neglect you?

He is thoughtful in all He created. Even the universe, which we know little about, shows His attentiveness to the works of His hands.

Psalm 147:4 (NKJV)
He counts the number of the stars; He gives names to all of them.

He not only placed each star in the sky but gave them each a name! Did you know that stars sing? *Job 38:7.* Wow! Just writing this has me awestruck! What about you? Can you see the magnitude of His wisdom and knowledge by simply observing His creation? We are talking about a God who tells the ocean when to turn back…the sun when to rise…He who has walked on the ocean floor!

As we meditate on God's omnipotence and now His omniscience, fear cannot stand a chance against this awareness of this wonderous God that welcomes you as a child of His and a friend of Jesus. What an honor to be called a child of such a God! I find it humbling.

Today's Promise

Do you not know? Have you not heard? The everlasting God, the Lord, the Creator of the ends of the earth does not become weary or tired. His understanding is inscrutable.
Isaiah 40:28

Questions

What part of Isaiah 40:28 most encourages you? Why?

_____

_____

_____

_____

_____

How does God's omniscience dispel fear?

_____

_____

_____

_____

Today's Prayer

Psalm 145:3 (NKJV)
Great is the LORD, and greatly to be praised;
and His greatness is unsearchable.

Dear Lord, as I think of all the amazing works of Your hands… a showcase of Your infinite knowledge, help me in the times that challenge my faith. I know You see me and have not grown tired or weak. I, however, find that times I do grow tired and weak. Please help me in my times of weakness. The times look bleak, but You are all-knowing, all-powerful, and in charge of everything. I turn my life over to You. Have Your perfect will in my life; I know you know what is best. Thank you so much for all the beautiful things You have made and done and are doing on my behalf. Keep me in Your precious hands.

Thoughts

_____

_____

_____

_____

_____

Group Study Questions

What are some of the things that cause us to lose sight of God's abilities?

What can we do differently to prevent this?

How does the knowledge of God's 'all-knowing' impact your life?

This All-knowing God is willing to be your counselor! Is there anyone who knows better than He what is best for you? How can this knowledge of God be put to use?

Day 5 - *Here... There... and Everywhere!*

When we think of God, it is easy to imagine Him high above the earth and far away - seated on a throne in heaven surrounded by angels with His son Jesus seated at His right hand. So, where *exactly* is that? Somewhere beyond our universe. Frankly, somewhere beyond our comprehension.

Hebrews 1:1-3 (NIV)
[1] In the past, God spoke to our ancestors through the prophets many times and in various ways,
[2] but in the last days He has spoken to us, by His son, whom He appointed heir of all things, and through whom also He made the universe.
[3] The Son is the radiance of God's glory and the exact representation of His being, sustaining all things by His powerful word. After he had provided purification for sins, He sat down at the right hand of the majesty in heaven.

So yes, we know that Jesus sits at the Father's right hand from Hebrews 1:3. Jesus ascended into the heavens in plain view of his disciples.

Luke 24:50-51 (NIV)
[50] And when He had let them out to the vicinity of Bethany, He lifted up his hands and blessed them.
[51] While He was blessing them, He left them, and was taken up into heaven.

Another account is found in Acts.

Acts 1:9 (NIV)
After He said this, He was taken up before their very eyes, and a cloud hid Him from their sight.

Today, we will explore God's omnipresent attribute and discover what that exactly means. Omnipresent is the ability to be everywhere at once. Let's look at what the Bible says about God's omnipresence.

Matthew 18:20 (NIV)
Where two or more are gathered in My name, there I am in the midst of them.

Mathew 18:20 are the words of Jesus himself. He is present when you pray with another person or persons and call on His name! Right there with you! That means He is capable of being in more than one place at a time. This is more challenging to wrap our minds around. Let's see what else the Bible tells us about this ability.

Proverbs 15:3 (NIV)
The eyes of the Lord are everywhere, keeping watch on the evil and the good.

Not only is He present in heaven and with those calling on His name, but all the while, He is capable of seeing everything going on: every hidden evil deed and every good deed being done on earth. *But wait... there's more...*

Isaiah 57:15 (NIV)
For this is what the High and Exalted One says-He who lives forever, whose name is holy: "I Live in a high and holy place, but also with the one who is contrite and lowly in spirit, to revive the

29

spirit of the lowly and to revive the heart of the contrite."

He lives in a high and holy place. This place where He dwells is far exalted above the earth. This high and holy place is His home. In this place is the holiness and glory of Yahweh (another name for God).

Some of the choices we make in life or the plights we may find ourselves in result in a state of brokenness. Yet this same God graciously chooses to be with the contrite. Contrite means broken, trodden down, crushed, and beaten, brought about by deep remorse, regret, and shame.

Let's be clear: just because someone is broken does not mean they are contrite or truly 'sorry.' Not all 'sorrys' are equal. I have met, over the years, many who are quick to say the words 'I'm sorry,' but often not for the right reasons. You've heard these types of apologies. You know, the ones that mean, *'I'll say I'm sorry so you will stop talking about it.'* Or, how about the *'I'm sorry'* - minus the rest of the sentence, *'I got caught.'* Let's not forget the 'sorry' that comes from the consequences that cost the person more than anticipated, yet void of remorse for the pain they caused someone else.

Lowly in spirit refers to a person broken and humbled by their awareness of their sin and unworthiness...a heart bearing the weight of guilt. God says for such a person He will revive-which means 'to make alive' and comfort them. It is comforting to know He will meet us where we are, even when we bring an adverse situation on ourselves. The key here is a genuinely repentant or contrite heart.

Jeremiah 23:23-24 (NKJ)

23 *"Am I only a God nearby," declares the Lord,*
"and not a God far away?"
24 *Who can hide in secret places so that I cannot*
see them?" declares the Lord. "Do I not fill
heaven and earth?" declares the Lord.

We can glean from this passage that God is both far and near. God, who must stay separate from us due to our sins and His holiness, chooses to draw near to us through His son, Jesus Christ, who broke the barrier of separation when he died on the cross.

As we explore God's omnipresence, I want to take this time to clear up some false inferences concerning His omnipresence.

Some believe that because God is everywhere, He is in everything. This belief is rooted in Pantheism. Pantheism is a doctrine that considers the universe conceived of as a whole as God and, conversely, that there is no God but the combined substance, forces, and laws manifested in the existing universe. This belief is a deviation from truth, though it has subtly made its way into many Christian circles due to many Christians not understanding fundamental Christian principles.

Yes, God is everywhere, but He is not in everything. Though God created the universe, He is not the universe. God shares many attributes with His creation, such as life. Just because God gives a tree life does not mean He is living in the tree. On the contrary, the tree is living because of God's generosity. The life He has chosen to share with the tree is only a portion of the life force that He is...hence, it is corruptible. He shares the breath of life with every living

31

thing because He chooses to. He is life, but that is not *all* He is. God is so much more than just life. He is holy, omniscient, omnipotent, omnipresent, and full of grace; he is Love and immeasurably more. Just as a tree is not omnipresent because it is alive, no more are we divine because God shared some of His attributes with us. Worshiping trees, the earth, the universe, or each other is worshipping the creation instead of the Creator.

So, let's say a person paints a beautiful picture and gifts the painting to a friend. Wouldn't it be odd for the friend to give thanks to the image and give kudos and honor to it for being beautiful? It would be equally as ridiculous to think that the picture is part of the giver of the gift or that the artist is somehow totally embodied in the object. Keep going with this line of thought, and that is where people come up with 'Why pray to God or even acknowledge Him for that matter? I should be praying to myself! I am equal to God...He is in me'. Anyone entertaining this thinking embarks on the same false pride that got Lucifer/Satan in trouble.

Satan has wanted the glory that belongs to God since before we existed. If he can confuse people into worshipping an object instead of God, he can position himself or his demons to be worshipped. The adversary is not omnipresent, but he does have many demons under his command. One-third of the angles were expelled from heaven with him. Without a clear understanding that God is the Supreme Being, the creator of all created things, infallible, incorruptible, and Sovereign, *which we are not*, we can be led into false doctrine.

Be cautious when you hear comments or greetings like 'The God in me sees the God in you.' Unless the person is filled with the Holy Spirit, there is no God in them... or at least not the God you think you are addressing. Again, we may have some attributes of God that He endowed us with, such as life, but make no mistake, that by no means makes us God.

So, let's get back to places where God resides, besides everywhere.

Psalm 22:3 (KJV)
But thou art holy, O thou that inhabits the praises of Israel.

God resides in the praises of His people. When we praise, whether in song, music, words, or through any of the various ways of praising, it causes God's presence to manifest. I characterize the experience as a showering down of His presence. So even though God is always near, when we praise, He allows His presence to be known in an almost tangible way. Some have the gift of visions and can see what I would call anointing and glory falling in the place where praise and worship are taking place. Others may feel the change in the atmosphere in the form of overwhelming joy, gratitude, weights or burdens lifted, or even the washing of one's soul, which often takes the form of uncontrollable crying or tears.

Today's Promise

"For I know the plans I have for you," declares the Lord, "Plans to prosper you and not to harm you, plans to give you hope and a future.

Jeremiah 29:11

Questions

Have you ever experienced a contrite heart?

_____

_____

_____

_____

_____

Has anyone ever given you what seemed like an apology that did not feel like an apology at all?

_____

_____

_____

_____

_____

How did that make you feel?

_____

_____

_____

_____

_____

Is there something you verbally repented of, but maybe not exactly from the heart?

_____

_____

_____

_____

Take a moment to ask the Lord to bring any offenses that you have not sincerely repented to your mind. Write them down.

_____

_____

_____

_____

Today's Prayer

Dear Lord Jesus. Thank you for this day you have allowed me to experience. Forgive me for the times I have not had a repented heart when I've offended you and others. Please show me the error of my ways so I can be pleasing in your sight. Teach me how to praise you in such a way that pleases you so I can experience your presence in a completeness that I've never experienced before. You're amazing!

Thoughts

_____

_____

_____

_____

_____

Group Study Questions

Have you ever experienced God's presence when praising and worshiping?

Have you ever experienced God's presence when you were not praising or worshiping?

How would you describe God's presence?

Share experiences you have had with apologies, sincere or otherwise.

How do you determine if an apology is sincere?

36

Day 6 - *The Ninth Hour*

Today, let's look at what took place the hour our Lord died on the cross.

45 From the sixth hour until the ninth hour, darkness came over all the land.

From what would be equivalent to 12 noon to 3 pm, the sun was not allowed to shine light! All Powerful God!

> *46 About the ninth hour, Jesus cried out in a loud voice, "Eloi, Eloi, lama sabachthan?"—which means, "My God, my God, why have you forsaken me?"*

Though Heaven is a destination we are excited about reaching one day, it can also seem so far away. Have you ever felt disconnected and alone? There are times on this journey when we all will or have felt this way at some point. Have you ever called out to God, and it seemed He was nowhere to be found? Jesus was not exempt from human experiences while He walked the earth. On the cross, Jesus had to endure the weight of our sins. The penalty of sin-crucifixion for crimes He did not commit, yet He chose to endure the pain and humiliation. Jesus gave us an example of how to handle the worst anguish imaginable.

Matthew 27:46 is often misunderstood. Some that teach the Bible teach that God turned His back on His son. It could seem that way going by the words "My God, my God, why have you forsaken me?" until you understand the origin of those words. Those words are a direct quote from Psalm 22:1. Jesus knew scripture and prophecy pertaining to His

37

destiny. In times of trouble, He relied on God's word. There is no doubt that when Jesus cried out, quoting Psalm 22:1, He referenced the entire passage. It was the custom among prophets and teachers to quote the first verse of a passage of scripture to reference the entire passage.

> [47] *When some of those standing there heard this, they said, "He's calling Elijah."*
> [48] *Immediately, one of them ran and got a sponge. He filled it with wine vinegar, put it on a stick, and offered it to Jesus to drink.*
> [49] *The rest said, now leave him alone. Let's see if Elijah comes to save him.*
> [50] *And when Jesus had cried out again, in a loud voice, He gave up His spirit.*

What had Jesus cried out again spoken of in the 50th verse? The answer is in the account of Luke.

Luke 23:46 (NIV)
And when Jesus had cried with a loud voice, He said. Father, into your hands I commit my spirit: and when He had said this, He breathed his last.

Does that sound like the words of someone who thought they were forsaken? Luke 23:46 reveals the final, tender words rendered by someone with total trust in whom they are talking. Though God allowed Jesus to feel the pain and anguish of sin, which resulted in feeling like He was separated from God, don't get it twisted; God by no means had forsaken Jesus. Nor did Jesus lose His faith in God's love for Him. God's presence never leaves us or forsakes us. There are times in our life that we will have to rely on what God has said... not what we may feel.

Matthew 27:51 (NIV)
*At that moment the curtain of the temple was
torn in two from top to bottom. The earth shook,
and the rocks split.*

The barrier of separation was represented by the veil (the curtain in the temple). The veil was blue at the top, representing the heavens, and the bottom red, representing humanity and the earth, the color of Judean hills. The blue and the red blended perfectly in the middle, creating purple (the color of royalty and Jesus's robe). The curtain was 30 feet high and 30 feet wide. The fabric's thickness is debated; some say 4 inches thick, while others say over 12 inches thick. What we do know for sure is that the veil was thick enough to completely conceal what was behind it: the Holy of Holies. Who but God could rip 30 feet of fabric from top to bottom at that exact moment? If the earth had ripped the curtain due to the earthquake, it would have been pulled apart from the bottom up, not from the top to the bottom. Remember, the curtain represented the separation of God's holiness from His sinful creation. By the death of Jesus, the veil or separation is removed. We now have a path back to God ... through His son.

Read Psalm 22

Psalm 22 (NIV)
[1] *My God, My God, why have you forsaken me?
Why are you so far from saving me, so far from
my cries of anguish?*
[2] *My God, I cry out by day, but you do not
answer, by night, but I find no rest.*
[3] *Yet you are enthroned as the Holy One; you are
the one Israel praises.*

39

⁴ *In you our ancestors put their trust; they trusted and you delivered them.*
⁵ *To you they cried out and were saved; in you, they trusted and were not put to shame.*
⁶ *But I am a worm and not a man, scorned by everyone, despised by the people.*
⁷ *All who see me mock me; they hurl insults, shaking their heads.*
⁸ *He trusts in the LORD," they say, "let the LORD rescue him. Let him deliver him, since he delights in him."*
⁹ *Yet you brought me out of the womb; you made me trust in you, even at my mother's breast.*
¹⁰ *From birth, I was cast on you; from my mother's womb, you have been my God.*
¹¹ *Do not be far from me, for trouble is near and there is no one to help.*
¹² *Many bulls surround me; strong bulls of Bashan encircle me.*
¹³ *Roaring lions that tear their prey open their mouths wide against me.*
¹⁴ *I am poured out like water, and all my bones are out of joint.*
My heart has turned to wax; it has melted within me.
¹⁵ *My mouth is dried up like a potsherd, and my tongue sticks to the roof of my mouth; you lay me in the dust of death.*
¹⁶ *Dogs surround me, a pack of villains encircles me; they pierce my hands and my feet.*
¹⁷ *All my bones are on display; people stare and gloat over me.*
¹⁸ *They divide my clothes among them and cast lots for my garment.*

¹⁹ But you, LORD, do not be far from me. You are my strength; come quickly to help me.
²⁰ Deliver me from the sword, my precious life from the power of the dogs.
²¹ Rescue me from the mouth of the lions; save me from the horns of the wild oxen.
²² will declare your name to my people; in the assembly I will praise you.
²³ You who fear the LORD, praise him! All you descendants of Jacob, honor him! Revere him, all you descendants of Israel!
²⁴ For he has not despised or scorned the suffering of the afflicted one; he has not hidden his face from him but has listened to his cry for help.
²⁵ From you comes the theme of my praise in the great assembly; before those who fear you I will fulfill my vows.
²⁶ The poor will eat and be satisfied; those who seek the LORD will praise him— may your hearts live forever!
²⁷ All the ends of the earth will remember and turn to the LORD, and all the families of the nations will bow down before him,
²⁸ for dominion belongs to the LORD and he rules over the nations.
²⁹ All the rich of the earth will feast and worship; all who go down to the dust will kneel before him— those who cannot keep themselves alive.
³⁰ Posterity will serve him; future generations will be told about the Lord.
³¹ They will proclaim his righteousness, declaring to a people yet unborn: He has done it!

Today's Promise

Let your conduct be without covetousness; be content with such things as you have. For He Himself has said, "I will never leave you nor forsake you."

Hebrews 13:5

Questions

What do we learn about the relationship of the Father and Son through the crucifixion event?

_____

_____

_____

_____

_____

How does their relationship affect you?

_____

_____

_____

_____

Thoughts

_____

_____

_____

Today's Prayer

Jesus, this day, I have an even deeper appreciation for the sacrifice you made for me. What an excellent example you set for us to rely on your word in the darkest hours of our lives. Help me not forget that you are ever present in our time of need; even if I cannot feel you near, remind me of your promises. Thank you, Heavenly Father, for making a path back to you through Your Son, my savior, Jesus Christ!

Group Study Question

Go through Psalm 22 verse by verse and identify all the verses that pertain directly to what Christ was going through on the day of the crucifixion.

Day 7 - *Connecting with God Through Prayer*

One of the most powerful tools we have as Christians is prayer. Prayer is a powerful tool that moves the hand of God. However, if what the Bible says about prayer is not clearly understood, we can find our faith being challenged. Today, we will examine what prayer is and some misconceptions of prayer.

I have heard people express -- far too many times -- how disappointed they are with God. More times than not, the disappointment stems from prayers that they feel went unanswered. Have you ever felt this way? Disappointment in relationships often occurs when people lack knowledge or understanding about someone, in this case, God, and consequently form unrealistic expectations.

The simplest definition of prayer, I would ascribe, is communicating with God. Talking to God, worshiping the Lord, praising God, and listening to God are all considered forms of prayer. Often, prayers include thanksgiving and requests. Requests can consist of the need for direction, wisdom, material needs, healing for yourself or others, salvation for loved ones, intercession for leaders, and so on. Though the list of things prayed about is endless, prayer usually falls into four basic categories:

- Prayers of blessing and adoration, which is praising God or worshipping him. This form of prayer can also be achieved through song.
- Prayers that are petitions such as asking for forgiveness, requests, or needs.
- Intercessory prayer is asking God for something on behalf of someone else.

- Prayers of thanksgiving are offered to God for what He has done or is doing.

Let's look at what God's word says about prayer so we can put it into perspective.

Mathew 7:7-8 (NIV)
[7] "Ask and it will be given to you; seek and you will find; and knock and the door will be opened to you.
[8] For everyone who asks receives; the one who seeks finds; and to the one who knocks, the door will be opened."

Matthew 21:22 (NIV)
And all things you ask in prayer, believing, you will receive."

John 14:13-14 (NIV)
[13] Whatever you ask in My name, that will I do, so that the Father may be glorified in the Son.
[14] If you ask Me anything in My name, I will do it.

These are some of the most frequently quoted verses in the Bible.

In the late 70s, a new dogma emerged and became immensely popular among many Christians. Some refer to this new philosophy era as the 'Name It - Claim It' doctrine. Many Christians embraced the idea that He will give you anything you ask of God (if you have faith). By reading what God says about asking and receiving in Mathew 7:7-8, Mathew 21:22, and John 14:13-14, one can quickly see how these verses give credence to the 'Name It - Claim It's assertion if not read in conjunction with other scriptures on the same topic. This loose interpretation and lack of understanding of scripture led to confusion, disappointment, and even loss of faith. People would be blamed for their own illnesses; being told they were not healed due to their lack of faith. Those seeking wealth were encouraged to keep naming and claiming prosperity or material things until they received whatever they desired. Again, if they did not receive what they were 'naming and claiming', the problem was attributed to their lack of faith.

Without a complete understanding of God's word about prayer, people often find themselves giving God orders and then disappointed when they find out God is not the 'Genie of the Lamp'... waiting to hear from them on what to do next.

Luke 11:5-13 (NIV)
5 Then Jesus said to them, "Suppose you have a friend, and go to him at midnight and say, 'Friend, lend me three loaves of bread,
6 a friend of mine, on a journey, has come to me, and I have no food to offer him."
7 And suppose the one inside answers, 'Don't bother me. The door is already locked, and my children and I are in bed. I can't get up and give you anything."
8 I tell you, even though he will not get up and give you the bread because of friendship, yet because of your shameless audacity, he will surely give you as much as you need.
9 So I say to you: Ask and it will be given to you; seek and you will find; knock, and the door will be opened to you.

> [10] *For everyone who asks receives; the one who seeks finds; and the one who knocks the door will be opened.*
> [11] *"Which of you fathers, if your son asks for a fish, will give him a snake instead?*
> [12] *Or if he asks for an egg, will give him a scorpion?*
> [13] *If you then, though you are evil, know how to give good gifts to your children, how much more will your **Father in heaven give the Holy Spirit to those who ask Him!***

In this passage, very similar to Matthew 7:7-8, it is made clear *what* God promises to give to those who ask, seek, and knock, which is the Holy Spirit.

There is no question that God wills for a person to have the Holy Spirit if that is their desire. Consequently, a person asking to receive the Holy Spirit does not cause a conflict between their will and God's will. The request of such a person is pleasing to God. Being a good Father, our God will not withhold any good thing from His children.

Let's take a look at a segment of the words of Jesus when asked by his disciples how to pray:

Matthew 6:9-10 (NIV)
> [9] *"This then, is how you should pray:*
> [10] *Our Father which art in Heaven, hallowed be thy name. Your Kingdom come, **Your will be done.** On earth as it is in heaven".*

Matthew 6:10 is the first line of what is often called the 'Lord's Prayer' (might be better named 'The Disciples Prayer' in that it was an answer to how the disciples should pray) …

47

a blueprint -- if you will. First, identifying where God resides, then acknowledging His name is holy (hallowed be thy name), we are then to pray for the coming of God's kingdom. His kingdom coming entails His will being done on earth the same way it is done in heaven. His will on earth or some translations read in earth, includes the details of our lives. We are clearly instructed to pray in God's will or said differently ... for God's will to be done.

1 John 5:14-15 (NKJV)

[14] *This is the confidence that we have in him, that if we ask anything, according to his will, he hears us.*

[15] *And if we know that he hears us, whatever we ask, we know that we have the petitions that we have asked of him"*

In the above passage, the promise of answered prayer again includes the word *if* (*a conjunction word that proceeds a conditional clause*). The condition to be met in this passage is praying in accordance with His will.

1 John 3:21-22 (NIV)

[21] *Dear friends, if our hearts do not condemn us, we have confidence before God,*

[22] *and receive from him anything we ask because we keep his commands and do what pleases him.*

In this passage, John uses the word "*if* " again in verse 21. So, in other words, as long as we have a clear conscience before the Lord, we can have assurance our prayers will be answered. Clear conscience refers to not living in a sinful state. Does this mean we never sin? Of course not! Not living in a sinful state refers to not having uncorrected and unrepented sinful *practices* in your life.

48

The word 'because' is a subordinating conjunction. Similar to the word 'if,' the term 'because' in verse 23 creates cause and effect (automatically making the first statement dependent on the other). Here, in the latter part of verse 23, we see that if we want the assurance of answered prayer, not only is it necessary to refrain from practicing sin, but also that we keep His commandments and do what pleases Him. This includes submitting our prayer to His will.

James 4:3 (NIV)

When you ask, you do not receive because you ask with the wrong motives, that you may spend what you get on your pleasures.

James 4:3 reveals yet another stipulation to answered prayer. Wrong motives, such as greed or lust for the things of this world, pride of the eyes, and so on, are also reasons your prayers may not be answered. Realizing the impact of wrongly motivated prayers offsets the theology that anything you are asking will be granted, thus substantiating the necessity of studying the scriptures. A complete knowledge of all or at least many scriptures on a particular subject gives a different and much clearer understanding of the writer's intent.

John 15:7-8 (NKJV)

[7] If you abide in Me, and My words abide in you, you will ask what you desire, and it shall be done for you.
[8] By this is my father's glorified, that you bear much fruit, so shall you be My disciples.

In verse 5 of John 15, Jesus speaks of himself being the true vine and we the branches. To abide in Him is to stay connected to Him and not live our lives apart from Him. Our choices in life should reflect His life, love, and strength operating in us and through us. If we are connected to Him, then His desires become our desires. When His word, which has the supernatural power and ability to change us from within, is part of you because you live by it and allow it to govern your choices, your prayers will align with His will. Your prayers will not be filled with selfish requests; instead, you will find yourself praying to benefit the kingdom of God and others.

As our lives begin to line up with God's word, our desires change. Consequently, what is essential to God becomes meaningful to us, significantly impacting our prayers. Praying in His will or for His will to be done affects our results.

How powerful are the promises we can stand on when we meet the necessary criteria? Keeping His commandments is how we abide in His love.

John 15:12 (NKJV)
"And this is my commandment, that you love one another as I have loved you."

A final note for the day... Therefore, God has the final say regarding our prayers, which should bring comfort, knowing God knows what is best for us and everyone involved. The answer to our prayer may be 'no' or 'not now.' This may not be the answer we want to hear, but it is still an answer, nonetheless.

Today's Promise

And this is the confidence that we have in him, that, if we ask anything according to His will, he heareth us:

1 John 5:14

Questions

Is there something specific you are believing in God for?

_____

_____

_____

_____

_____

If so, are you praying that His will be done?

Is there anything that is not pleasing to God that you are holding on to that may be hindering your prayers?

_____

_____

_____

_____

_____

Today's Prayer

Dear Lord Jesus, I desire to abide in You and You in me. Bring to my mind anything unconfessed and unrepented sin that I may have forgotten so that I can bring it to you and therefore be in right standing with you. As I am learning more about Your word, I ask that You transform me with the power of Your word. Let my heart align with your heart so my prayers will be in harmony with You and answered. Help me remember and believe you know what is best for me. You know the concerns of my heart. Thank you for the privilege of calling on your name. Use me, Lord, to bless someone in this day.

Thoughts

_____

_____

_____

_____

_____

Group Study Questions

Why is praying in God's will so important?

Have you or anyone you know been affected by the 'Name it - Claim it' teaching?

What examples can you think of where scripture is taken out of context?

Day 8 - *Meditation*

In today's society, the line between Christianity and paganism is often blurred. Not too different from biblical times, the church finds subtle and not-so-subtle infiltration of pagan practices. Even something as basic as the definition of prayer has been convoluted in many churches. We've taken a closer look at what the Bible says about prayer on day 7, identifying some misconceptions. Today, we are going to take a look at meditation.

All five major religions – Hinduism, Buddhism, Judaism, Islam, and Christianity practice meditation. Though many believe that meditation practices began in India, evidence places its origin in Egypt. These practices were adopted by neighboring countries and spread throughout the world. Many Christians today have embraced meditation and incorporated the techniques into their lives, unaware of biblical guidelines concerning meditation.

There are many forms of this ancient practice. Meditation is a method used to connect to the spiritual realm, found in the 'Great Nothingness'. It is believed that focusing one's mind for a period but not engaging with thoughts (also known as emptying the mind) evokes relaxation and a variety of other benefits, including a state of blissfulness. Where the world is offering bliss, the Word of God is offering peace.

Isaiah 26:3 (NKJV)
You will keep him in perfect peace, Whose mind is stayed on you, because he trusts in You.

The world's point of view is that peace can only be felt or attained when there is no conflict. Jesus provides us with inner peace, even in the midst of a battle - not predicated on circumstances or putting our minds to sleep. The Lord's peace through His gospel is peace despite our circumstances.

Getting to the state of mindlessness through meditation is achieved in silence or with the help of chanting. Chanting puts the mind into an altered state of conscience, similar to sleep. Our mind is the gatekeeper of our temple, which is our body. Is having the guard or gatekeeper of the temple in an altered state of conscience a good idea? When the gatekeeper is not on guard, it is an opportunity for anything to enter. The Spirit of God does not enter by taking advantage of an altered state of mind. However, don't count on other deceiving spirits to be so gracious.

Proverbs 4:23 (NIV)
Above all else, guard your heart, for everything you do flows from it.

Proverbs 4:23 (NKJV)
Keep your heart with all diligence, For out of it spring the issues of life.

Psalm 1:1-3 (NIV)
¹ Blessed is the man who walks not in the council of the ungodly, or stands in the path of sinners, nor sits in the seat of the scornful;
*² But his delight is in the law of the Lord, **and in his law, he meditates day and night**.*
³ He shall be like a tree planted by the rivers of water, that brings forth its fruit in its season, whose leaf also shall not wither; and whatever he does shall prosper.

We are told in God's word to guard our minds and hearts by being intentional about our thoughts. That is the opposite of emptying your mind. The Bible is very clear about meditation... what we are to meditate on. Meditation on anything but God's word can be dangerous. Opening one's self up to, or attempting to make contact with, the 'spiritual realm' while putting the mind in an altered state can invite demonic activity into one's life. Such practices are not supported by scripture.

Many people today confuse prayer with meditation or believe they are synonymous. They are not the same. Prayer is communication with God, while meditation (without guidance from God's word) does not embrace or consist of any moral belief system.

Just to be clear, meditation, reflection, and contemplative 'prayer' is not the same use of the word prayer when the Bible speaks of prayer or praying. Emptying your mind (a form of meditation often confused with prayer due to the clever title it's been given – 'contemplative prayer') and many meditation techniques taught today that have infiltrated the church are contrary to what the Bible tells us.

Even meditating on God, Jesus, or the Holy Spirit should be scripture-based. Meditating on scripture, whether a verse or passage, is to give thoughtful consideration to the meaning or implication of the scripture. The Holy Spirit will often speak to us when meditating on His word, offering deeper insight and a more meaningful experience in God's word.

Psalm 1:2 (NKJV)
His delight is in the law of the Lord, and in His law does he meditate day and night.

Psalm 119:15-16 (NKJV)

15 *I will meditate on Your precepts and contemplate Your ways.*
16 *I will delight myself in Your statutes; I will not forget Your word.*

*Thinking about God or remembering things about Him differs from talking to Him. Though reflection can stir a person to prayers of thanksgiving and reminiscing on the goodness of God (*which we are encouraged to do*), reflection of itself is not prayer.

Today's Promise

You will keep him in perfect peace, whose mind is stayed on you; because he trusts in you.

Isaiah 26:3

Questions

Why is it important to meditate on God's word?

_____

_____

_____

_____

_____

What are some of the ways you can guard your mind?

_____

_____

_____

_____

_____

Why is guarding your mind so important?

_____

_____

_____

_____

Today's Prayer

Dear Lord Jesus, thank you for this day you have allowed me to be a part of. Thank you for your grace in these confusing times. These times are so full of deception that it has become hard to distinguish truth from lies. Increase my discernment so I will not be deceived. Forgive me for anything I may have entertained that was not pleasing to you. Help me recognize the subtle thoughts that come into my mind that are in opposition to your word. Guide me this day and allow me to share your truth with someone.

Thoughts

_____

_____

_____

_____

_____

Group Study Questions

What are some of the ways we can distinguish truth from lies?
Have you experienced non-Christian practices in church?

Discuss yoga as a group. Should yoga be considered paganistic or not?

Why or why not?

Day 9 - *The Sin Factor*

Welcome to Day 9! Look at God! You've made it to Day 9, so you're still on your journey to spiritual growth! Today, we will look at the struggle *we all* have with sin.

To address this topic, we need to identify what sin is. Sin is defined as an immoral act considered a transgression of divine law. There are three categories sin falls into:

- Sin of commission – Thoughts, words, and deeds that violate God's divine law and commandments.
- Sin of omission – Failure to obey...not doing the right thing you know to do.
- Unpardonable sin – blasphemy against the Holy Spirit. Attributing the work of the Spirit to Satan.

More than a few people refuse to accept the reality that "all have sinned". They struggle with the concept of repentance. Often, this mindset is rooted in pride. Any bad they have done is somehow justified, either not *that bad* or someone else's fault.

Then, we have those who argue that we are born 'good' and that our nature is basically good. According to this theory, people are tainted by their environment, which turns them from their essential good to a not-so-good nature.

The Bible says the opposite. Jesus says in Luke 18:19, "No one is good except God alone."

1 John 1:8 (NIV)
If we say we have no sin, we deceive ourselves, and the truth is not in us.

It is hard for some to reconcile that even a sweet baby (often called 'A Little Angel') could have a sinful nature. However, anyone who has been around children can recognize their rebellious ways and how quickly they choose disobedience over obedience. Yes, even babies, given a chance, will twist your face, pull your hair, and throw a bottle at you - testing the boundaries. As a young parent, I thought my new *'little darling'* must be just developing his motor skills and had very little control of his muscles *until the bottle hit me in the head!* The sooner the parent figures out that their little darling knows precisely what they are doing, the better off everyone will be. Humans' propensity towards rebellion, selfishness, and unkindness shows as soon as they are able to physically demonstrate their will.

So then, how did sin become such a dominating force in our lives? Let's look back at where it all began.

Genesis 1:26-27 (NIV)
26 *Then God said, "Let us make mankind in our image, in our likeness, so that they may rule over the fish in the sea, the birds in the sky, over the livestock, and all the wild animals, and over all the creatures that move along the ground."*
27 *So God created mankind in his own image, in the image of God, he created them; male and female, he created them.*

This passage shows us that God created the first man and woman in His image. Image is referring to physical similarities. The 'likeness of God' refers to the spiritual attributes of the moral character of God. Adam and Eve were given a Godly nature, notwithstanding the privilege of exercising free will.

60

Geneses 3 (NIV)

[1] *Now the serpent was more crafty than any of the wild animals the LORD God had made. He said to the woman, "Did God really say, 'You must not eat from any tree in the garden'?"*

[2] *The woman said to the serpent, "We may eat fruit from the trees in the garden,*

[3] *but God did say, 'You must not eat fruit from the tree that is in the middle of the garden, and you must not touch it, or you will die.'"*

[4] *"You will not certainly die," the serpent said to the woman.*

[5] *"For God knows that when you eat from it your eyes will be opened, and you will be like God, knowing good and evil."*

[6] *When the woman saw that the fruit of the tree was good for food and pleasing to the eye, and also desirable for gaining wisdom, she took some and ate it. She also gave some to her husband, who was with her, and he ate it.*

[7] *Then the eyes of both of them were opened, and they realized they were naked; so they sewed fig leaves together and made coverings for themselves.*

[8] *Then the man and his wife heard the sound of the LORD God as he was walking in the garden in the cool of the day, and they hid from the LORD God among the trees of the garden.*

[9] *But the LORD God called to the man, "Where are you?"*

[10] *He answered, "I heard you in the garden, and I was afraid because I was naked; so I hid."*

¹¹ *And he said, "Who told you that you were naked? Have you eaten from the tree that I commanded you not to eat from?"*

¹² *The man said, "The woman you put here with me—she gave me some fruit from the tree, and I ate it."*

¹³ *Then the LORD God said to the woman, "What is this you have done? "The woman said, "The serpent deceived me, and I ate."*

¹⁴ *So the LORD God said to the serpent, "Because you have done this, "Cursed are you above all livestock and all wild animals! You will crawl on your belly and you will eat dust all the days of your life.*

¹⁵ *And I will put enmity between you and the woman, and between your offspring and hers; he will crush your head, and you will strike his heel."*

¹⁶ *To the woman he said, "I will make your pains in childbearing very severe; with painful labor you will give birth to children. Your desire will be for your husband, and he will rule over you."*

¹⁷ *To Adam he said, "Because you listened to your wife and ate fruit from the tree about which I commanded you, 'You must not eat from it,' "Cursed is the ground because of you; through painful toil you will eat food from it all the days of your life.*

¹⁸ *It will produce thorns and thistles for you, and you will eat the plants of the field.*

¹⁹ *By the sweat of your brow you will eat your food until you return to the ground, since from it you were taken; for dust you are and to dust you will return."*

²⁰ Adam named his wife Eve because she would become the mother of all the living.
²¹ The LORD God made garments of skin for Adam and his wife and clothed them.
²² And the LORD God said, "The man has now become like one of us, knowing good and evil. He must not be allowed to reach out his hand and take also from the tree of life and eat, and live forever."
²³ So the LORD God banished him from the Garden of Eden to work the ground from which he had been taken.
²⁴ After he drove the man out, he placed on the east side of the Garden of Eden cherubim and a flaming sword flashing back and forth to guard the way to the tree of life.

Sin entered the world through Adam's choice to disobey God... corrupting Adam. Thus, sin affected every human being born after that. All people are born with a sinful nature and a natural propensity to sin. I like to call it 'a sinful DNA'. We are wired to be immoral and born to die, as death entered the world due to sin.

Genesis 5:3 (NIV)
When Adam was 130 years old, he had a son in his own likeness, after his own image; and he named him Seth.

Every son and daughter born to Adam and Eve no longer had the benefit of being created in the likeness of God but instead born in the likeness of Adam - *contaminated* Adam – a sinner. Adam, being no longer divine (*in the likeness of God*), Adam could not pass the 'likeness of God' to his offspring. The seed of Adam was now and evermore corrupted by sin.

Romans 5:12 (NIV)
"Sin entered the world through one man, and death through sin, and in this way death came to all people, because all sinned"

We qualify as sinners in two ways: we practice sin and are born with a sinful nature inherited from Adam. When we add the fact that an evil prince of darkness rules this world and perpetrates sin, it would seem we are in pretty bad shape. Sin separates us from God and has an erosive effect on our conscience, making it easier and easier to persist in sin. Sin diminishes our sensitivity towards others. Even guilt, which initially acts as a deterrent from sin, eventually poses no threat to evil when sin is practiced long enough.

Psalm 19:12 (NIV)
Who can discern his own errors? Cleanse me from my hidden faults.

Today, let's take a few minutes to identify any sinful behavior or attitudes you may be harboring in your heart. Sometimes, unrepented sin can be hidden from our consciousness. Unforgiveness is a common sin that is easy to overlook. Offenses done to others are another area where sin can linger unnoticed. Ask the Lord to reveal to you any hidden sin that may be loitering in the chambers of your heart.

1 John 1:8-9 (NIV)
[8] *If we say we have no sin, we deceive ourselves, and the truth is not in us.*

[9] *If we confess our sins, He is faithful and just to forgive us our sins and cleanse us from all unrighteousness.*

Repenting is not a 'One and Done'. Daily, we sin in one way or another. We constantly offend, and though the blood shed on the cross has covered our sins, we still need to repent often.

Psalm 103:8 (NIV)
The Lord is merciful and gracious, Slow to anger, and abounding in mercy.

Today's Promise

If we confess our sins, He is faithful and just to forgive us our sins and to cleanse us from all unrighteousness.
1 John 1:9

Questions

Do you relate to anything about Eve and Adam's choice to sin?

_____

_____

_____

_____

_____

Can you think of sinful hereditary traits or tendencies common to your family?

_____

_____

_____

_____

_____

Today's Prayer

Psalm 51: 1-13

[1] *Have mercy upon me, O God, According to Your lovingkindness; According to the multitude of Your tender mercies; Blot out my transgressions.*
[2] *Wash me thoroughly from my iniquity, and cleanse me from my sin.*
[3] *For I acknowledge my transgressions, and my sin is always before me.*
[4] *Against You, You only, have I sinned, and done what is evil in your sight – that You may be found just when You speak and blameless when you judge.*
[5] *Behold, I was brought forth in iniquity, and in send did my mother conceive me*
[6] *Behold, You desire truth in the inward parts, and in the hidden part You will make me to know wisdom.*
[7] *Purge me with hyssop, and I shall be clean; Wash me, and I shall be whiter than snow.*
[8] *Make me hear joy and gladness, that the bones You have broken, may rejoice*

⁹ Hide Your face from my sins, and blot out all my iniquities.
¹⁰ Create in me a clean heart, O God, and renew a steadfast spirit within me.
¹¹ Do not cast me away from your presence, and do not take your Holy Spirit from me.
¹² Restore to me the joy of your salvation, and uphold me by Your generous Spirit.
¹³ Then will I teach transgressors Your ways, and sinners shall be converted to You.

Thoughts

_____

_____

_____

_____

_____

Group Study Question

Why do you think it is so hard for some people to repent?

What was Eve's first mistake?

What do you think of Adam's response when confronted by God?

Day 10 - *Overcoming the Power of Sin and Temptation*

Though Jesus overcame sin and death for all who believe in Him, we will still have the sin issue to deal with as long as we are in these bodies of flesh where sin resides. Because Jesus defeated death and conquered sin, when you became a Christian, you became part of Christ. As a part of Christ, you share in His past victories... His crucifixion, His burial, and His rising from the dead. This means you, too, are now dead to sin and no longer controlled by its power.

Galatians 2:20 (NIV)
I have been crucified with Christ, and I no longer live, but Christ lives in me. The life I now live in the body, I live by faith in the Son of God, who loved me and gave himself for me.

John 3:5 -7 (NKJV)
⁵ Jesus answered, "Most assuredly, I say unto you, unless one is born of water and the Spirit, he cannot enter the kingdom of heaven.
⁶ That which is born of the flesh is flesh, and that which is born of the Spirit is spirit.
⁷ Do not marvel that I said to you, 'You must be born again.'

When we have received the Spirit of Christ, sin no longer has dominion over us. We have the power to resist.

James 1:14-15 (NIV)
¹⁴ Each one is tempted when, by his own evil desire, he is dragged away and enticed.

¹⁵ *Then, after desire has conceived, it gives birth to sin; and sin, when it is full-grown, gives birth to death.*

Let's look at the five stages of sin defined in James 1:14-15

- The first stage of the sin process begins with a person's evil desire. Evil desire is any ungodly desire that can be found in the flesh. These desires entice us as they war against God and His law. This conflict between our desires and God's commandments is a constant battle due to our sinful DNA.
- Stage 2 is the point where evil desires conceive. This is where uncorrected sinful thoughts and desires gain power as we agree or consent. Evil desire becomes alive in us.
- Next step, stage 3, sin is born. It has passed the point of being a passing thought and now is rooted in you and taking on a life of its own. The sin now has a form that can be recognized and begins to manifest outwardly. The book of Genesis describes it as an 'entity crouching at the door'.
- Once sin has taken root, it continues to grow. Stage 4, we see that sin is rarely confined to the origin in which it began. Its un-confined tentacles reach into different areas of our life.
- The final stage of sin is death. Death in scripture often refers to separation from God and physical death.

The good news is that we can overcome sin by the power of the Holy Spirit! Though it is an ongoing process, His Spirit will give you strength in the face of temptation. He will help you recognize thoughts that lead to sin so they can be stopped at the door of your mind and not allowed to get to stage one of the sin process.

Jesus, when tempted in the Judean Desert, gave us a great example of what tool to use. He combated sinful suggestions and temptation by using God's word to shut it down.

Luke 4:1-13 (NKJV)

¹ *And then Jesus, being filled with the Holy Spirit, returned from the Jordan, and was led by the Holy Spirit into the wilderness,*

² *being tempted for 40 days by the devil. And those days He ate nothing, and afterward, when they had ended, he was hungry.*

³ *the devil said to Him, "If you are the son of God, command the stone to become bread."*

⁴ *But Jesus answered Him, saying, "It is written, 'Man shall not live by bread alone, but by every word of God.' "*

⁵ *Then the devil, taking Him up on a high mountain, showed him all the kingdoms of the world in a moment of time.*

⁶ *And the devil said to Him, "All this authority I will give you, and their glory; for this has been delivered to me, and I give it to whomever I wish.*

⁷ *Therefore, if you will worship before me, all will be Yours."*

⁸ *And Jesus answered and said to him, "Get behind Me, Satan! For it is written, 'You shall worship the Lord, your God, and Him only you shall serve.'"*

⁹ *Then he brought him to Jerusalem, set Him on the pinnacle of the temple, and said to him, "If*

you are the Son of God, throw Yourself down from here.
^{10} For it is written: 'He should give his angels charge over you, to keep you
^{11} and, 'In their hand they shall bear you up, lest you dash your foot against a stone,'"
^{12} Jesus answered and said to him, "It has been said, 'You shall not tempt the Lord your God.'"
^{13} Now when the devil had ended every temptation, he departed from him until an opportune time.

Note how Jesus was filled with the Holy Spirit and led by the Holy Spirit. The Holy Spirit will remind you of scripture in times of temptation. This is just one of the reasons being Spirit-filled is critical to the fight against sin.

John 14:26 (KJV)
But the Comforter, which is the Holy Ghost, whom the Father will send in My name, will teach you all things, and bring all things to your remembrance whatsoever I have said unto you.

The Holy Spirit will bring back to your memory God's word, but note… memory. In other words, it is a prerequisite to have heard or read His word for it to be a memory. This is why hearing the preached word and reading His word is so important. It is a significant tool that can disarm the adversary and your natural bend toward sin. Once God's word is embedded in you, the Holy Spirit can access God's powerful word to shut down the power of temptation. Speak God's word against sinful thoughts and see how fast they dissipate!

More great news! This is cause to rejoice!

2 Corinthians 12:7-9 (NKJV)

[7] *And lest I should be exalted above measure by the abundance of the revelations, a thorn in the flesh was given to me, a messenger of Satan buffet me, let's I'd be exalted above measure.*
[8] *Concerning this thing I pleaded with the Lord three times that it might depart from me.*
[9] *And He said to me, **"My grace is sufficient for you, for My strength is made perfect in weakness"**.*

Yes, we are sinners... but sinners SAVED BY GRACE! Even with failures on our journey to victory, His grace is enough to sustain us! An inexhaustible supply of grace is more than enough to maintain and sustain the promise of salvation. The Lord will take the opportunity to show His strength when we are weak, so there be no mistake - All the Glory belongs to God!

Today's Promise

No temptation has overtaken you that is not common to man. God is faithful, and he will not let you be tempted beyond your ability, but with the temptation he will also provide the way of escape, that you may be able to endure it.

1 Corinthians 10:13

Questions

Can you remember a time when uncorrected sin in your life led to different stages of sin?

_____

_____

72

_____

_____

_____

How can you combat sinful thoughts?

_____

_____

_____

_____

How does hearing and reading God's Word assist the Holy Spirit?

_____

_____

_____

_____

Can you think of hereditary sinful traits particular to your family?

_____

_____

_____

_____

Today's Prayer

Dear Lord God of Heaven and Earth. I praise your name! Thank You for what You went through to overcome the power of sin and death on our behalf. As I learn more about You daily, let what I know about You take root in me. I desperately want to be more like you. Holy Spirit, fill me and take control of my life. I know you have already defeated sin. Please help me to keep the sinful nature in me to stay dead by not giving in to the temptation to act in ways that gratify my sinful nature or the flesh. Thank You for your GRACE!

Thoughts

_____

_____

_____

_____

_____

Group Study Questions

Share a time when God's strength showed up in your weakness.

Share ways sin has affected the world.

Day 11 - *First Steps Toward Healing*

In the following two lessons, we are going to talk about healing. Recognizing the need for healing does not always constitute a person's desire to be healed. The road to recovery, for many people, starts when the need for healing is recognized, followed by a sincere desire to be healed.

I knew a woman for many years who was tormented by the memories of her past. Her past was horrific by no fault of her own. She was a prisoner of her past. Following her tumultuous childhood, her life significantly improved, yet the damage done in her youth made it difficult... if not impossible, for her to enjoy her current circumstances. Her past was a crippling force in her life. The unforgiveness she harbored against her father bled into the unforgiveness of multiple people throughout her lifetime. She led an emotionally isolated life. She struggled with love... not free to show it or receive it. She would often rehearse the worst parts of her life in her tormented mind or with specific people she chose to share it with. I was one of the people she confided in.

As life moved on, four children later and a marriage of fifty years, one day after listening again to her rehearse her negative past, I decided to take a different approach on this occasion. I told her she needed to forgive those she was harboring malice towards. She answered, "She could not forgive." I then asked her if she wanted to forgive and start on a road to healing. I told her if she wanted to be healed, God would help her to forgive. There was a long pause. Finally, she answered, "I'll get back to you on that." Here is a classic example of how a person may recognize they need healing but may not necessarily want to be healed. In her case, she eventually got to the point of wanting healing, but it was several years later.

In the 5th chapter of John, there is an account of a man in need of healing. Let's look closely at his response:

John 5:1-16

¹ And after this, there was a feast of the Jews, and Jesus went up to Jerusalem.

² Now there is in Jerusalem, by the sheep gate, a pool, which is called in Hebrew, Bethesda, having five porches.

³ In these lay a great multitude of sick people, blind, lame, paralyzed, waiting for the moving of the water.

⁴ For an angel went down at a certain time to the pool, and stirred up the water; then whoever stepped in first, after the stirring of the water, was made well of whatever disease he had.

⁵ Now a certain man was there who had an infirmity 38 years.

⁶ When Jesus saw him lying there, and knew that he already had been in that condition a long time, He said to him, "Do you want to be made well?"

⁷ The sick man answered him, "Sir, I have no man to put me into the pool when the water is stirred up; but while I am coming, another steps down before me."

⁸ Jesus said to him, "Rise, take up your bed, and walk."

⁹ And immediately the man was made well, took up his bed, and walked. And that day was the Sabbath.

¹⁰ The Jews, therefore, said to the man who is cured, "It is the Sabbath; it is not lawful for you to carry your bed."
¹¹ He then answered them, "He who made me well said to me, 'Take up your bed and walk.'"
¹² Then they asked him, "Who is the man who said to you, 'Take up your bed and walk'?"
¹³ But the man who was healed did not know who it was, for Jesus had withdrawn, a multitude, being in that place.
¹⁴ Afterward, Jesus found him in the temple and said to him, "See that you have been made well. Sin no more, less the worst thing come upon you."
¹⁵ The man departed and told the Jews that it was Jesus who had made him well.
¹⁶ For this reason the Jews persecuted Jesus, and sought to kill Him, because He had done these things on the Sabbath.

Looking deeper into this account, consider key points often missed when reading the story.

First of all, when Jesus, in verse 6, asked the man if he wanted to be healed, the man did not answer the question; instead, he offered a reason why he wasn't healed. If you had a sickness of some sort and a person asked you if you wanted to be healed, would you readily say yes? Apparently, yes is not as certain an answer as might be expected. It is fair to assume that this man went to great lengths to get to the healing waters. It would appear to any person, looking on, that he wanted to be healed. However, ask yourself... would you come to the healing waters without the help you need to get into the water? I can't say definitively about this man in particular, how sincere he was about his healing; however, some people go to great lengths to give an impression that may or may not be the whole truth.

The next thing worth noting is Jesus heals the man, and yet there is no record of the man thanking Jesus or even asking for Jesus's name. Was the man a narcissist, or perhaps he hadn't decided if he was grateful? Maybe the man didn't want to be healed. Could it be possible that life depended on others was preferred to carrying his own weight? Getting a job? Being responsible for his own needs? Hmm. The answer to this is that we may never know for sure. Look at what happens next...

What happens next is interesting. Jesus runs into the man at the temple and warns him to sin no more before something worse happens to him. This comment indicates that the man had done something that brought the ailment or judgment on himself in the first place. It had been 38 years of deserved punishment. So, what does the man run out and do? (*Mind you, this is a week later, as he is utilizing the benefits of the healing he received from Jesus*). He goes out of his way to find the Jewish leaders to identify Jesus by name. The persecution against Jesus increased following the actions taken by this man to identify Jesus. Jesus knew what kind of man this was and still chose to show him mercy and grace. This man did not change or seem too thrilled about being healed. He had just been warned to stop sinning and yet went out of his way to cause harm to someone who had shown him kindness. This contemptuous effort to harm Jesus suggests he did not place much value on his healing. When I read this account, I couldn't help but wonder what became of this man. Hit by a bus? Oh, that's right... no buses. Maybe run over by a camel. Who knows. Whatever happened, I'm pretty sure it didn't end well.

Sometimes, we do not recognize our need for healing. Here, I've listed a few tell-tale symptoms that may indicate the need for healing:

- Trouble sleeping
- Anxiety
- Constant sadness
- Consumed by negative thinking
- Angry
- Over-reaction to adverse situations
- Inability to foster relationships
- Impatient and irritable
- Nightmares or flashbacks of traumatic experiences
- Failure to trust people, even those who have proven trustworthy

Many of these symptoms can directly result from unforgiveness, traumatic experiences, or both.

It is God's will that we be made whole. I pray that if there is brokenness within you, God reveals the areas that need repair and gives you a willing heart to seek Him for healing.

Today's Promise

who himself bore our sins in His body on the tree that we having died to sin might live to righteousness; by whose stripes you were healed.

1 Peter 2:24 (NKJV)

Questions

Do you recognize any of the symptoms listed above as an ongoing issue for you? If so, which ones?

_____

_____

_____

_____

_____

Do you know someone with these characteristics?

_____

_____

_____

_____

_____

If yes, how did you react to them in the past?

_____

_____

_____

_____

_____

How would you react today to someone with these characteristics? Would you do anything different today?

_____

_____

_____

_____

_____

Do you need a healing?

_____

_____

_____

_____

Are there memories you can't recall without fresh emotion coming to the surface? If so, write them down.

_____

_____

_____

_____

Today's Prayer

Dear Lord. You know me. If I need healing, please make it clear to me. Please do not allow me to go on any further in life in denial or oblivious to my need for help. If not, please help me recognize someone else's needs so I can pray for them. Help me not to take it personally when hurting people, hurt people, but instead, be compassionate and loving. Let me be a part of someone else's healing by allowing me to be a conduit of Your love by Your Spirit.

Thoughts

_____

_____

_____

_____

_____

Group Study Questions

Why do you think the man went out of his way to identify Jesus to His enemies?

Why do you think the woman was unsure if she wanted to be healed?

Have you ever met someone like her?

Day 12 - *Next Step to Healing*

Welcome back! In the previous lesson, we discussed the first step to healing: recognizing the need for healing. I pray that if you need healing, it has been made clear to you. The next step is answering the question, 'Do you want to be healed?' As ridiculous as this question may seem, it might surprise you how many people, though they may say they want to be healed, have not made that decision.

We are born into a broken world, and most people have encountered brokenness in one form or another. This world has endless ways to create spiritual and emotional brokenness, which can lead to or contribute to physical brokenness.

Some have embraced their condition for various reasons. Some have lived so long in a broken state that they fear being whole. Perhaps, for some, it seems easier to remain broken than to start the healing process. Let's not neglect to mention those whose need for attention - any attention - is so great that any form of it will do. Some will even live a miserable life to induce pity from others (another form of attention). There is no limit to what some will do for attention, like an unquenchable thirst.

To those of you who have embraced your condition, perhaps given up hope that your plight can be improved, I pray that you will find the courage to hope again as I write this. God can heal you in the broken areas of your life. Ask Him and let Him! He can restore you! He is a healer! He can recover you from the damage this world has done. He can heal you from the trauma you may feel you can't get past. He can heal your mind. He can heal your broken heart.

Maybe you have a fear of facing the world unbroken. Have you built a wall around yourself? Due to the pain of rejection or betrayal, have you isolated yourself so long that you believe you no longer would know how to interact with other people in a positive way, much less trust them? You may have concluded that you are better off not allowing anyone to get close to you. Nothing in and nothing out! For you, I pray right now, as you are reading this, that God will deliver you from the prison that you have found yourself in.

Like most people, I have had my share of betrayal, letdowns, and disappointments in relationships. This I want to share with you; it was life-changing for me:

Praying one day, I told the Lord I could no longer trust the people who had hurt me. His answer was as clear as if He was standing next to me. He said, "I didn't tell you to put your trust in people... trust me." That revelation has helped me deal with many of life's disappointments. There is nowhere in God's word that He tells us to put our trust in people, not even 'Christians'. I am by no means implying that there shouldn't be a level of trust in relationships. I am just reminded that all too often, our expectations of humans would be better balanced if we remember *we all have a sin nature.* There is no need to isolate; just be mindful of what the Bible says about people, and you won't be so vulnerable. Disappointed at times? Probably. But devastated? *No.* We are all flawed in one way or another and have disappointed someone at some point in our lives; it would serve us well to remember this. Or maybe not you, just the rest of us. ☺

To those who just don't want to start the healing process, believing it's too much work, I understand. You've tried to convince yourself that you are no longer affected by hurts from your past, yet you know the very thought of specific experiences is as upsetting as if it was happening right then. Here is the truth: the most challenging part of this journey is deciding to take it.

Don't be deceived or intimidated by the enemy with lies he will try to fill your mind with. 'Too hard, too long, too late, I am too messed up, I can't be healed.' Don't believe it! The Devil is the father of lies. Many people are in bondage just because they believe his negative narrative. Know this... *You are NOT beyond God's reach!*

Isaiah 59:1 (NIV)
Surely the arm of the Lord is not too short to save,
Nor His ear too dull to hear.

Psalm 145:18-19 (NIV)
[18] *The Lord is near to all who call on Him,*
to all who call on Him in truth.
[19] *He fulfills the desires of those who fear Him;*
He hears their cry and saves them.

During the few years I had the privilege of working at Patrick Airforce Base, a privilege because I consider it an honor to serve people who sacrificed a great deal for what they believed. I spoke with many retired veterans and active-duty soldiers in all military branches. Managing the base barbershop gave me a rare opportunity to have candid, what I would call interviews with the men and women who came in. Many shared with me some of the terrible ordeals they had gone through.

One such interview was with a man I'll refer to as John. I asked John how he was able to deal with the terrible memories that haunted him. He replied, "I put them in a box in my mind. I try to rarely open the box. If I were to open it, I fear what may come out." For many people, the healing journey appears to be too painful. The fear of revisiting traumatic memories is too daunting a task, almost a feeling that coming anywhere near the subject would cause 'the dam to break'... the only thing holding back complete destruction. Again, don't believe the lie. You can be healed. Ask the Lord to heal you. Some may find Christian counseling a tool God uses to help you. Ask the Lord to lead you to the right counselor if that is the route you are directed to take. Just know this: the moment you seek God for help, He will help you. The healing is internal, so don't be surprised if it takes time. Be patient. Again, let God do what only God can do.

Here is an important key. When we are struggling with something, God often allows adverse circumstances to continue so that we can learn to trust and depend on Him. One of the main ways of exercising our trust in Him is demonstrated when we express a heart of gratitude no matter how difficult things may be at the time. Learn to practice thanking God in the good times and bad. Play uplifting music that reminds you of the goodness of God; it can help redirect your focus. Until you learn to believe and trust that He sees you, loves you, and will take whatever you are going through to use for your ultimate good, you may find that you remain in the circumstance longer than necessary.

Isaiah 41:10 (NKJ)
"So do not fear, for I am with you; for I am your God. I will strengthen you and help you; I will uphold you with my righteous right hand."

John 14:27 (NKJ)
Peace I leave with you, My peace I give unto you; not as the world gives, give I unto you. Let not your heart be troubled, neither let it be afraid.

Psalm 23:4 (NKJ)
Though I walk through the valley of the shadow of death, I will fear no evil, for you are with me; your rod and staff, they comfort me.

The Shepherd carefully and thoughtfully navigates the sheep through dangerous territory. Jesus is the 'Good Shepherd'.

Lastly, there are those of you who have such a self-esteem deficit; you not only cling to negative situations but often will help to create such circumstances. If things are not 'bad' enough... you will find a way to make it worse. This behavior often stems from neglect and abuse in the foundation of your upbringing...damaged people... damaging people. Those in this state will often attempt to invoke pity from others to influence or force - if you will - people to care for them. This behavior stems from the belief that they are unloved and unvalued. Though positive affirmations can undoubtedly help, they only help for a limited time, kind of like a band-aid that doesn't stick for long. It takes God to heal and seal what seems to be a well with no bottom.

If the person I just described resonates with you, even in part, ask the Lord to plant the scriptures below in your heart. His supernatural Word will transform you. Yes! You can be healed by the renewing of your mind!

Ephesians 2:10 (NLT)
For we are God's masterpiece. He has created us a new in Christ Jesus, so we can do the good things He planned for us long ago.

You are indeed a masterpiece! Yes, You! When you accepted Jesus Christ as your savior, you were made new. Whatever negative narratives you have been conditioned to believe about yourself is no longer who you are. I pray that you will begin seeing yourself as God sees you. "Wonderfully and beautifully made!" I believe that as you read this, God will start healing you. Remember, it is a process. You are not relying on positive affirmations from the world to heal the brokenness; instead, the amazing supernatural power of His word to transform.

Jeremiah 31:3 (NIV)
"I have loved you with an everlasting love; I have drawn you with unfailing kindness."

Oh, how He Loves You! You are not forgotten, not an afterthought of God. You are so valuable that He left heaven to die a terrible, tortuous death so you can have eternal life. The mere fact that this book has made it to your hands manifests His care for you. I am praying that you will experience His love and that it will heal your heart and replace the negative opinions you have adopted about yourself (what you have been conditioned to believe) with what God says about you!

Today's Promise

He will wipe every tear from their eyes. There will be no more death" or mourning or crying or pain, for the old order of things has passed away.

Revelations 21:4

Questions

Can you identify an area in your life where you may need healing?

_____

_____

_____

_____

_____

Describe yourself as if you were telling someone who has never met you about you.

_____

_____

_____

_____

In your own words, what does God say about you?

_____

_____

Does what God says about you concur with how you see yourself?

Today's Prayer

Jesus, Jesus, Jesus. There is no name above your name. Your name is exalted above the heavens and the Earth. Today, Lord, I am coming to you, asking you to examine me. As you examine me and you see the hidden areas of my life, the scars, the tears, the brokenness, I am asking you, Dear Lord, to begin the healing process in me. Reveal the areas where I am broken to call them out specifically and lay them at your feet. I acknowledge that you are a healer, for you are my creator. I desperately need you to make me whole to be all you intended me to be. I want to live without fear, without insecurity, without anxiety. I am ready to be healed. I acknowledge that healing can be found in you and will come from you. I cannot heal myself. Thank you, Lord, for beginning the healing process within me as of this very day. Amen

Thoughts

_____

_____

_____

_____

_____

Group Study Questions

What are signs that may indicate a need for healing?

What are signs that God is healing you?

What do you do when you encounter broken people?

Day 13 - *Blessing Blockers*

Glad you have made it this far. Welcome to day 13. Today, I want us to take a look at blessing blockers. Have you sought God for healing, peace, intervention in the lives of loved ones, or perhaps provisions, employment, or blessing over your business, yet it seems your prayers are not answered? Is it possible to block blessings? Yes, it is possible to block your own blessings. For the next two days, we are going to look at a variety of blessing blockers. Today, we are going to focus on unforgiveness.

Harboring unforgiveness is one of the most destructive choices a person can make. If you don't forgive, you won't be forgiven.

Mathew 6:14-15 (NKJV)
14 For if you forgive men their trespasses, your heavenly Father will also forgive you.
15 But if you do not forgive men their trespasses, neither will your Father forgive your trespasses.

Who among us can afford the consequence of not being forgiven?

However, in addition to not being forgiven, which is not a position you want to find yourself in, unforgiveness is also a blessing blocker. When we don't forgive, we are withholding grace. Take a look at a parable Jesus shared:

Mathew 18:21-35 (NKJV)
21 Then Peter came to him and said, "Lord, how often shall my brother sin against me? Up to seven times?"

²² Jesus said to him, "I do not say to you, up to seven times, but up to seventy times seven.

²³ Therefore, the kingdom of heaven is like a certain king who wanted to settle accounts with his servants.

²⁴ And when he had begun to settle accounts, one was brought to him, who owed him ten thousand talents.

²⁵ But as he was not able to pay, his master commanded that he be sold, with his wife and children, and all that he had, and that payment be made.

²⁶ The servant, therefore, fell down before him, saying, 'Master, have patience with me, and I will pay you all.'

²⁷ Then the master of that servant was moved with compassion, released him, and forgave him the debt.

²⁸ "But that servant went out and found one of his fellow servants who owed him a hundred denarii; and he laid hands on him and took him by the throat, saying, 'Pay me what you owe!'

²⁹ So his fellow servant fell down at his feet and begged him, saying, 'Have patience with me, and I will pay you all.'

³⁰ And he would not but went and threw him into prison till he should pay the debt.

³¹ So when his fellow servants saw what had been done, they were very grieved and came and told their master all that had been done.

³² Then his master, after he had called him, said to him, 'You wicked servant! I forgave you all the debt because you begged me.

³³ Should you not also have had compassion on your fellow servant, just as I had pity on you?'

^{34} *And his master was angry and delivered him to the torturers until he should pay all that was due to him.*
^{35} *"So My heavenly Father also will do to you if each of you, from his heart, does not forgive his brother his trespasses."*

It is a sin not to forgive. Often, we don't forgive because we think forgiveness is undeserved. Forgiveness is an act of grace. By definition, grace is **unmerited** favor. Failure to extend grace to one another is offensive to God. The grace that has been extended to us has in no wise been earned, much less deserved.

Not only can we block a blessing, but we can lose our blessings. In this parable, the man who owed the master ten thousand talents, equivalent to *160,000 years of wages...* a debt impossible to pay, was forgiven his entire debt; I think we can safely call that a blessing. So, what happened next? This man was owed one hundred denarii by someone, which was equivalent to *4 months of wages*. The man shows no grace or compassion to the man in debt to him. Instead, he behaves cruelly. The master finds out and is not happy; he comes after him for everything he had forgiven the cruel servant. This man's actions resulted in his blessing being rescinded. God has blessed you abundantly; let's keep that in mind when it is time to be gracious to someone else.

Releasing forgiveness brings a blessing of its own. As a bonus, you will experience healing and peace in place of anger and bitterness.

Ephesians 4:26-27 (NIV)
[26] *"Be angry, and do not sin": do not let the sun
go down on your wrath,*
[27] *nor give place to the devil.*

Psalm 4:4 (NIV)
*Be angry, and do not sin. Meditate within your
heart on your bed, and be still.*

The word "angry" is used in both of these passages. Unlike the English word, angry, the Hebrew word for anger means to be moved, disturbed, thrown into commotion, or disquieted as a result of anger, fear, or grief. When confronted with what we perceive as an attack, threat, or loss, we all are vulnerable to an immediate rise in emotion. The key is to hold your peace or restrain your anger; control your temper. Giving in to anger for just a moment can change the course of your life forever. Having an emotional reaction is not where sin is born. What we do about how we feel is where sin can get in.

The adversary tries to take full advantage of us when we are in a heightened state of emotion. He will tempt us to dwell on an offense, harbor unkind thoughts of resentment, and often encourage revenge. We are urged to let our anger go before we sleep at night. Make a conscious effort to forgive. Think about the day's events as you lay in bed and your emotions begin to subside. Seek objectivity. Ask the Lord for His peace and pray for the offender. Examine your heart to be sure you are not in any way guilty of wrongdoing. If so, repent quickly and sincerely. Don't offer yourself excuses. Just own any part you may have in the offense. On judgment day, we will be held accountable for our actions.

The offenders will be held accountable for theirs. What someone may have done or not done will not exempt you from what you did about it. "*I did not forgive because he or she...*" will not exonerate you in the eyes of God. This is how we don't give place to the devil; we offer him no opportunity to influence us. Ask the Lord to help you to let go and forgive. Heal my wounds.

Just a note... a good description of unforgiveness – drinking poison and expecting the other person to die.

Try this instead:

Romans 12: 17-21 (NIV)

[17] *Do not repay anyone with evil for evil. Be careful to do what is right in the eyes of everyone.*
[18] *If it is possible, as far as it depends on you, live at peace with everyone,*
[19] *Do not take revenge, my dear friends, but leave room for God's wrath, for it is written: "It is mine to avenge; I will repay, says the Lord.*
[20] *On the contrary: "If your enemy is hungry, feed him; if he is thirsty, give him something to drink. In doing this you will heap burning coals on his head."*
[21] *Do not be overcome by evil, but overcome evil with good.*

When we act in love, even if we are not feeling loving, the emotion will eventually follow.

Today's Promise

"If You, Lord, should mark iniquities, O Lord, who could stand? But there is forgiveness with You, that You may be feared."

Psalm 130: 3-4

Questions

Is there someone that you have not forgiven? If so, write down the offense.

_____

_____

_____

_____

_____

Is holding onto the offense worth the consequences that follow?

_____

_____

What action can you take to forgive if the person is still living?

_____

_____

_____

_____

_____

What action can you take to forgive if the person is deceased?

_____

_____

_____

_____

_____

I suggest writing a letter to the offender, spelling out the offense, and then releasing forgiveness for each offense. Even if the offender is deceased, write the letter and ask God to honor it and forgive you for the sin of unforgiveness.

Today's Prayer

Dear Lord, I have been forgiven for many offenses, yet I struggle to forgive others who have offended me. I acknowledge that unforgiveness is a sin, and I need Your grace as I, this day, choose to let go of past hurts and forgive those who have trespassed against me. I also pray for the ones that have offended me, that your grace, mercy, and blessings not be withheld from them. Please remove bitterness from my heart and heal and restore me. Thank you for being a good and gracious God, slow to anger and quick to forgive. I want to be more like you. Help me also to be slow to anger and quick to forgive.

Thoughts

_____

_____

_____

_____

_____

Group Study Questions

In the parable above, who does the master represent?

How have you seen unforgiveness affect your life? If not you, someone else.

How is forgiving tied to grace?

What is the best thing to do when you are offended?

Day 14 - *More Blessing Blockers*

I want you who are taking the time to do this Bible study to experience victory in all areas of your life. For this reason, I will take more time on blessing blockers. I want to expose things that could hinder God's blessings in your life.

Sin, of any kind, in our life can block blessings. Living in a sinful lifestyle, practicing sin, indulging in sinful behavior, and sexual immorality are just some of the easy-to-identify blessing blockers.

Earlier in this study, we have established that we all have a sin problem that is a daily battle. The daily struggle with the flesh is different for everyone. For some, it may be anger management; for others, it may be discipline; some wrestle with chronic complaining, while another's struggle may be laziness. The list of the traits or tendencies we battle to overcome in our daily walk is endless. The daily battle with our sin nature is not the same as living in a sinful arrangement or practicing sin habitually and not repenting and correcting it.

What constitutes unrepented sin? No shame, no remorse, or inclination to turn from it. Those who continue in this way will be treated as the wicked. Here is what can be expected:

Proverbs 13:21
Evil pursues sinners, but to the righteous, good shall be repaid.

Hidden sin in our lives will also block blessings. There are many Christians who have hidden sin in their lives. Pornography is a clear example of a secret sin among

100

Christian men and women. Look at these staggering statistics.

Christian men (ages 31 to 49):

- 77 percent looked at pornography while at work in the past three months
- 64 percent view pornography at least monthly.
- 18 percent admit being addicted to pornography (and another 8 percent think they may be).

Married Christian men:

- 55 percent look at pornography at least monthly.
- 35 percent had an extramarital affair.

Women are not exempt. 87% of Christian women have admitted watching porn. This is a prevailing and spreading problem for God's people. Because pornography is so easy to hide and is often followed by shame, confessing it or seeking help is often not pursued. Hidden sin can be the reason a person cannot prosper.

Proverbs 28:13 (NIV)
Whoever conceals their sins does not prosper,
but the one who confesses and renounces them
finds mercy.

This next blessing blocker may surprise a few of you. For married people, how you treat one another can impact your blessings.

1 Peter 3:7 (NIV)
7 Husbands, in the same way, be considerate as
you live with your wives, and treat them with

101

respect as the weaker partner and as heirs with
you of the gracious gift of life so that nothing will
hinder your prayers.

If your prayers are being hindered, your blessings are being blocked. Husbands and wives, it will serve you well to strive to be on one accord in your marital relationship. Mistreating each other is displeasing to God.

Laziness can block blessings. I've encountered people who want the benefit of wealth but are unwilling to work. They expect that God will give to them out of His wealth when, in fact, God expects us to use the talents He has given us, and He will bless our efforts.

Proverbs 10:4 (NIV)
Lazy hands make for poverty, but diligent hands
bring wealth.

Pride can be a very subtle sin. Pride can seep in unnoticed. We can start out humble and end up proud and arrogant. I know because it happened to me. God made a way for me to buy my first business when I was 22. I was utterly dependent on God for everything. I remember asking the Lord if I could make $10.00 that day to feed my younger brother and me, Taco Bell. God always provided. As time went on, God began to bless the business. Many years later, I had three locations and was doing exceptionally well. At first, my focus on ministry became marginally compromised, but over time, unperceived by me, my focus began to transfer from God to work goals. Now, don't get it twisted; if anyone asked about the business, I would give God the glory and acknowledge Him as having blessed the company. We, as Christians, can be on 'auto response'.

You know what I mean… 'God is good all the time' followed by 'and all the time God is good!'. How many people say this without a thought about the goodness of God? Many. How can I say this? By simply observing people's actions. If a person were mindful of the goodness of God, it would be evident in their speech and conduct. Rhetoric (language designed to have a persuasive or impressive effect on its audience but often regarded as lacking sincerity or meaningful content).

To make a long story short, I found myself far from the relationship I once had with God. I became so proud and arrogant that God stepped in and brought me back to square one because He loves me enough to correct me. Ouch! And even with that, it took years to recognize the magnitude of pride that had found a home in me. God had given me all the talent and success I had. He created me with specific talents, blessed my efforts, and granted me favor. Where I lacked knowledge or skill, the Lord, by His Spirit, directed me. Somehow, I lost sight of this, just as Lucifer did. He was so beautiful and talented that he lost sight of the fact that he did not create himself. Yeah…that part. Lucifer was a creation made by God to worship and serve Him. To God be all the Glory, Honor, and Praise! We are nothing without God.

Proverbs 16:18 (NIV)
Pride goes before destruction, and a haughty spirit before a fall.

Pride can cause you to lose blessings and block new blessings from coming. God would prefer to take you down a notch than to allow your heart to be corrupted by pride.

Just a few more blessing blockers, and we'll move on. One very common blessing blocker is selfishness, stinginess, and greed. If you are not willing to bless others, don't be surprised if God does not bless you. Oh, I'm not saying you won't acquire wealth; you very well may. There are many other blessings besides what you accumulate that are even more valuable than wealth. Health, peace, joy, and true friends are the start of the list of things money can't buy.

Luke 12:13-21 (NIV)

[13] *Someone in the crowd said to Him, "Teacher, tell my brother to divide a family inheritance with me."*

[14] *But He said to him, "Man, who appointed Me a judge or arbitrator over you?"*

[15] *Then He said to them, "Beware, and be on your guard against every form of greed; for not even when one has an abundance does his life consist of his possessions."*

[16] *And He told them a parable, saying, "The land of a rich man was very productive.*

[17] *And he began reasoning to himself, saying, 'What shall I do, since I have no place to store my crops?'*

[18] *"Then he said, 'This is what I will do: I will tear down my barns and build larger ones, and there I will store all my grain and my goods.*

[19] *'And I will say to my soul, "Soul, you have many goods laid up for many years to come; Take your ease, eat, drink, and be merry."'*

[20] *"But God said to him, You Fool! This very night your soul is required of you; and now who will own what you have prepared?*

[21] *So is the man who stores up treasure for himself, and is not rich toward God."*

The man in this parable showed no regard for God or anyone else. We are encouraged to be a conduit with the blessings God has given us. All we have is because of God and belongs to God. He entrusts us with whatever portion He sees fit. The more you give, the more will be given to you. When you get to heaven, it will matter how generous you have been on earth.

Hebrews 13:16 (NIV)
"And do not forget to do good and to share with others, for with such sacrifices, God is pleased."

Proverbs 11:24 (NIV)
One person gives freely, yet gains even more;
Another withholds what he should give and only
suffers want.

Final blessing blocker for the day. Think about how unmotivating it is to give to an unappreciative person who complains about what you haven't given them without acknowledging all you have done for them. Being ungrateful does not inspire God or anyone else to do more.

Gratefulness, thanks, or thanksgiving is mentioned 157 times in the Bible. Jesus is recorded giving thanks to the Father on seven different occasions. Let's not forget how offensive it is to God when we are ungrateful. This is a definite blessing blocker.

Romans 1:21-22 (NIV)
*[21] For although they knew God, they neither glorified Him as God nor **gave thanks to Him**, but their thinking became futile and their foolish hearts were darkened.*

^{22} *Although they claimed to be wise, they became fools.*

Many scriptures tell us to give thanks to the Lord. Think of yourself as a parent. How long would you keep giving to your child if they were unappreciative? Wouldn't it be more important to teach them appreciation than to continue trying to appease an unthankful heart? God loves us, but a lack of gratitude says all He has done for us is not enough. He willingly gave His life so we could live eternally.

1 Thessalonians 5:18 (NIV)
Give thanks in all circumstances; for this is God's will for you in Christ Jesus.

No matter your circumstances, God has already proven His love and faithfulness to you. Praise Him for all He has already done, and maybe...just maybe, He will be willing to do even more. God responds well to praise and acknowledgment.

Today's Promise

Command those who are rich in this present world not to be arrogant nor to put their hope in wealth, which is so uncertain, but to put their hope in God, who richly provides us with everything for our enjoyment.

1 Timothy 6:17

Questions

What blessing blockers may be blocking you?

_____

_____

_____

_____

_____

Write at least ten things that God has done for you. Think of the life-impacting blessings He has done for you.

_____

_____

_____

_____

_____

Today's Prayer

Dear Lord Jesus. Forgive me for (*name any unconfessed sin in your life or practiced sinful behavior*). I want to be in right standing with you in all areas of my life. Not just so my blessings are not blocked but because you have already done so much for me. I am grateful and owe you my life, love, and all. Thank you for everything you have done, are doing, and will do.

Thoughts

_____

_____

_____

_____

_____

Group Study Questions

What other blessing blockers can you think of?

Give examples of hidden sins.

What can we do to counteract the impact of sin?

Day 15 - *Riding the Grace Train*

What does the Bible say about grace? Most Christians are familiar with specific passages on this subject, but let's look at grace closely, specifically, God's grace. Grace and mercy are often mentioned together, so let me ensure we understand the difference. By definition, grace is unmerited favor, so how does this look in our lives? In simplest terms, we receive what we do not deserve. Mercy, however, is not receiving what we do deserve.

- Example of Grace: God allows you into heaven by no merit of your own

- Example of Mercy: You are not condemned to hell though guilty of sin

Ephesians 2:8-9 (NIV)
[8] *For it is by grace you have been saved, through faith – and this is not of yourselves, it is a gift of God –*
[9] *not by works, so that no one can boast.*

The grace we have received is a gift from God. A significant part of the gift of grace is salvation. Salvation is the deliverance or rescue from the consequences of our sin by removing sin. However, the benefit of grace continues beyond there. Once we receive the gift of salvation by grace, our relationship with God is changed, our spiritual condition is changed, and our eternal future is changed. Even the rights of the adversary's dominance in your life are broken and changed forever.

Changed relationship with God:

Galatians 4:7 (NIV)
*So you are no longer a slave; but God's child,
and since you are His child, God has made you
also an heir.*

What a blessing to be called His child! To be treated as a son or daughter of God is quite a privilege.

God has opted to share His wealth with Us! Just as a good father takes pleasure in sharing his wealth with his children.

Acts 20:32 (NKJV)
*And now I commend you to God and to the word
of His Grace, which is able to build you up
and to give you the inheritance among all those
who are sanctified.*

1 Peter 1:4 (NKJV)
*To an inheritance that is imperishable, undefiled,
and unfading, kept in heaven for you,*

How do we know we are children of God?

Romans 8:16 (NIV)
*The Spirit himself bears witness with our spirit
that we are children of God,*

Your past is erased, your present is now in the process of being restored to spiritual health, and your future is secured: eternal life.

Many of us are very familiar with Romans 8:1, though often only half of the verse is quoted.

Romans 8:1 (NIV)
Therefore, there is no condemnation to those who are in Christ Jesus,

How often do we hear the rest of it?

who do not walk according to the flesh but according to the spirit.

Having our sins forgiven means we are no longer condemned for our sins. Our sin has been blotted out. Imagine a report being done on your life, thousands of pages recording every deed. Every thought. Every word spoken. Actions, choices, and reactions you have yet to remember are recorded in the report on you. Then, one day, you come to know Jesus in the pardon of your sins, and the entire report is altered. If I were looking through the report on my life, I can only imagine how many parts of the report would have needed to be redacted.

In light of this great gift of salvation, I would be amiss if I did not remind us that our lives should not reflect a misunderstanding of God's grace. I find many Christians today no longer see sin as a serious problem. They treat sin as trivial in light of God's grace. Just because God is willing to forgive our sins, this by no means suggests that God takes sin lightly.

God took sin so seriously that He sent His own son to sacrifice His life to make forgiveness possible.

John 3:16 (NKJV)
For God so loved the world, that He gave His only begotten son that whosoever believed on His name should not perish but have everlasting life.

Yes, salvation is free. So once repentance and acceptance of Jesus Christ as the Son of God and your Lord and Savior has occurred, you have received the gift of salvation. Many become a 'Christian' merely for what I call 'fire insurance'. They understand that to escape the penalty of hell, they must be saved; however, believing that Jesus is the son of God who came to earth and died for your sins and following Jesus are two different things. Remember, the demons in hell believe. They know exactly who Jesus is but do not choose to serve him. It is entirely possible to know that Jesus is the son of God without accepting the gift of salvation. I have met many people over the years who will say they are Christians but are totally comfortable in an utterly sinful lifestyle, practicing sin. There is no sign of repentance or sign of awareness of their sin. When you talk with them, they quickly quote scriptures about grace but very little about what it costs to remove their sins. They seem to believe that once they've said the magic words (the prayer of salvation), they are now safely on the '*grace train*' and will not have to pay any penalty for their sin.

I am not in a position to judge what this type of person's soul condition is. What I do know is that there are still consequences to sin. If you continue in a sinful habit, for example, alcoholism, you can expect to end up with cirrhosis of the liver. You can also expect that your behavior will continue to damage the lives of those around you- including yourself. Continuing this practice may cost you your family, friends, and job.

Being forgiven does not mean we are not called to live a holy life. Like anyone else, Christians often fall in many areas; the key is that we are expected to get up and do better. Doing better could even mean that it's a process that may take time as we struggle with bad habits or strongholds in our lives; however, not attempting to overcome temptation or giving in to temptation without remorse may be a reflection of a non-repentant heart.

Though our sins have been forgiven, the consequences of sin are not usually removed while we are living out this life. Sin is very serious – the impact often lasts our lifetime and sometimes the lifetime of generations to come. Yes, God is merciful and will sometimes restore some of what was lost due to our tarrying in sin; because He is compassionate, He will also help us carry the burden we created, but some things are just plain not retrievable. For example... lost time. One of the most valuable commodities we have on earth - *if not the most-* is time. Once we have used time, it cannot be retrieved.

In just a few years, a child can go from a baby to an adolescent - from a teen to an adult. If you are not there in those precious years of a child's life (where you can establish Godly principles by your teaching and example), these years cannot be retrieved by showing up 20 years later. Am I saying you cannot have a relationship with that person after 20 years or more of absence? Of course not, but the impact you could have had in molding them will not be the same.

Sin will detain or prevent a person from attaining God's plan for their lives. Many blessings available to people are missed while they are detained, gratifying their sinful nature.

Taking communion often helps us remain mindful of the price paid for our sins to be forgiven. Remembering how our Lord suffered as He bore our sins should be sobering when we find ourselves tempted to sin.

Today's Promise

Let us then approach Cod's throne of grace with confidence so that we may receive mercy and find grace to help us in time of need.

Hebrews 4:16

Questions

Do you have the assurance that you are a child of God? Why?

_____

_____

_____

_____

_____

Have you ever taken grace for granted?

_____

_____

_____

_____

_____

Why is sin grave?

_____

_____

_____

_____

_____

Today's Prayer

Dear Lord, thank you for the marvelous gift of salvation.
Forgive me for the times I've taken sin lightly, undermining
the extreme cost you paid for me to be forgiven. Holy
Spirit, keep me ever mindful of the suffering unto death
you endured for me.

Thoughts

_____

_____

_____

_____

_____

Group Study Questions

Is the prayer of 'Salvation' fire insurance?

What happens to salvation if a Christian falls back into sin?

What are the consequences of sin?

Day 16 - *Is Attending Church Necessary?*

As times are rapidly changing, many people - including Christians, have been struggling with whether attending church in person is a part of the lifestyle they desire to continue. Perhaps you, like many others, have been struggling with the question, "Is church attendance necessary to maintain a relationship with God?". During the COVID years, when attending church was no longer an option, many churchgoers sought alternatives to in-person fellowship, while many others have been seeking alternatives to the traditional once-a-week gathering for years. Whether televangelist or online church services, many churchgoers have decided other means of service to be more convenient.

Are you among the many disillusioned with the traditional church for various reasons such as scandals, fallen leadership, hypocrisy, inconsistencies, questionable financial practices, and offenses? This growing trend to withdraw from the church is alarming, especially among younger generations. Others argue they can read their Bible and praise and worship on their own....no need to go to a building to do that.

I have been told on far too many occasions that the Church is just no longer relevant. I heard it said on a television network that football is the new 'Sunday service.' What about this one? "Why not spend Sunday morning praising God on the golf course? It's all the same if you think about God". But is it the same?

A person can start by dedicating their time on the golf course on a Sunday morning to a 'time spent with God.' I just wonder how long it will take before it changes from '*Time with God on the golf course'* to just simply *'Sunday morning golf'*. In the assembly of believers, it would not be so easy for the purpose of your presence to be lost.

Let's explore what God's word says on this subject. Is attending church service really a mandate? And if so, why? Why would it matter whether or not you participated in a church versus watching your favorite minister on the Internet… at a time more convenient for you? Is there a difference between attending a church in person versus an Internet Zoom meeting, conference call, or Skype meeting?

Let's start by identifying the term "church" in the New Testament.

The Greek term *ekklesia* is the translation for "church" as used in the New Testament. This term is used to identify the community of those who believe in Jesus Christ. The literal translation means assembly, meeting, or congregation. To be clear, in the New Testament, no temple, tabernacle, chapel, synagogue, or any other meeting place was ever called church. The term always referenced Christian assembly. In the New Testament, it was used for the local community of believers and the overall group of Christians. Today, the term usually refers to the actual place of gathering or the body of believers as a whole.

Hebrews 10:24-25 (NIV)
[24] *And let us consider how we may spur one another on toward love and good deeds,*
[25] ***not giving up meeting together,*** *as some are in the habit of doing, but encouraging one another - and all the more as you see the Day approaching.*

Even as the Church was in the earlier stages of growth, there were those who habitually did not meet or assemble with other believers. Perhaps not so different from today, they lacked the understanding of the value of coming together with other believers.

Attending a place where Christians gather (often called a church) is strongly encouraged, though not mandated. It is a place where we inspire one another to do the right thing, encourage and be encouraged, meet one another's needs, admonish and be admonished. Hearing the word of the Lord through His minister strengthens and builds faith. Many churches also offer prayer, whether for healing, restoration, salvation for a loved one, finances, or any other of the numerous prayer requests. Here is an opportunity to have many stand with you in petitioning the Lord. Church is also the number one place to bring someone to hear the message of salvation. More people respond to the call of salvation in a church than anywhere else.

Matthew 18:19 (NKJV)
Again, I say unto you, that if two of you shall agree on earth as touching anything that they shall ask, it shall be done for them of my Father which is in heaven.

Romans 12: 4-8 (NIV)
[4] *For just as each of us has one body with many members, and these members do not all have the same function,*
[5] *so in Christ we, though many members, form one body, and each member belongs to all the others.*

118

⁶ We have different gifts, according to the grace given to each of us. If your gift is prophesying, then prophesy in accordance with your faith; ⁷ if it is serving, then serve; if it is teaching, then teach; ⁸ if it is to encourage, then give encouragement; if it is giving, then give generously; if it is to lead, do it diligently; if it is to show mercy, do it cheerfully.

Actual in-person fellowship is essential, if not critical, to our spiritual growth.

We are the body of Christ. Christ is the head of the Church, and we are members of one body. In order for the Church to operate the way God designed it, everyone needs to do their part. We have all been given different gifts to edify or benefit the body of believers, but how is that possible if *you* are not there?

With that said, unfortunately, many churches have become like sporting events. Most look on as spectators, while a small few perform. Those spectating desperately need the exercise, while those on the field are exhausted and need a break. I urge you to seek out a church where you are encouraged to discover your spiritual gifting and allowed to develop and use your gifts; doing this will help you mature in Christ.

God inhabits the praise of His people. When we come together in praise and worship, His presence is present. Yes, we can praise and worship alone, but it is not the same as worshiping collectively with other believers. God makes His presence known powerfully and unmistakably when we praise him corporately.

119

Over the years, I've heard people commenting about the service, such as - "I didn't really get anything out of church today." Or, have you heard this one? "They didn't sing any of the songs I like, so I wasn't really 'feelin' it." Attending service should not just be about what we can get but what we can bring. If you walk into church with a mindset to bring something to the service, it will definitely have an impact on your experience.

Galatians 6:2 (NKJV)
"Bear one another's burdens, and so fulfill the law of Christ."

Here's a thought...see anyone you don't recognize? Maybe someone who seems troubled? Welcoming strangers or offering a kind word or a listening ear to a hurting person are examples of how we can add to the service.

1 Thessalonians 5:11 (NIV)
Therefore encourage one another and build up one another, just as in fact you are doing.

We can strengthen one another by simply reminding someone of God's love, sharing a testimony, or reinforcing God's faithfulness. Again, you must be present to be available to the various ways God can use you to strengthen or build up His people.

Praying for the service, the leadership, and those trying to get to service that may be being hindered is helpful, not just to the body of believers but to you as well. It gets your mind focused where it ought to be. This can be done before church, just as you enter, or during the service.

I remember sitting in a church service when suddenly it seemed the pastor speaking went off course...like suddenly he lost his thoughts. He kept talking but finally just dropped his head. I discerned he was struggling. Immediately, I prayed that the Holy Spirit would help him. The pastor, at the very moment the prayer ended, lifted his head and said, "Thank you. Someone just prayed for me. Thank you!" Whether it was my prayer or many prayers that intervened at that moment, the power of prayer worked. He was able to finish his sermon without any more derailments. Much better response than talking about how 'the pastor seemed off today'.

Just a side note:

When you put yourself in a place where God can speak to you (such as an assembly of believers) and where you can be a blessing to someone else, even times when you think or feel as though you are not receiving anything, God will be pleased with you just for being obedient and available. Often, even if you cannot identify any 'takeaways' from the sermon, His spirit within you has been strengthened merely by being in the presence of God and other Spirit-filled people.

Mathew 18:20 (NKJV)
For when two or three are gathered together in my name, there am I in the midst of them.

If you or anyone you know has forsaken gathering with God's people, I urge you to reconsider or encourage that fellow believer to reconsider that decision.

Psalm 100 (NKJV)

¹ Make a joyful shout to the Lord, all you lands!
² Serve the Lord with gladness; Come before His presence with singing.
³ Know that the Lord, He is God; it is He who has made us, and not we ourselves; we are His people and the sheep of His pasture.
⁴ Enter into His gates with thanksgiving and into His courts with praise. Be thankful to Him, and bless His name.
⁵ For the Lord is good; His mercy is everlasting, and His truth endures to all generations.

Praising and worshiping the Lord in the company of other believers is an honor and a privilege. As crucial as fellowship is, do understand that circumstances can prohibit one's ability to fellowship in person.

Ephesians 2:8-9 (NKJV)

⁸ For by grace you have been saved through faith, and that not of yourselves; it is the gift of God,
⁹ not of works, lest anyone should boast.

In conclusion, you will not lose your salvation by not attending service; however, staying connected to a church family is biblically recommended to aid in your spiritual development. The Spoken Word feeds our souls. If you go too long without spiritual food, you become more vulnerable to the enemy's attacks and loss of faith.

Today's Promise

"Trust in the Lord with all your heart and lean not on your own understanding; in all your ways submit to Him and he will make your path straight."

Proverbs 3:5-6

Questions

Have you lost your enthusiasm for attending church or gathering with other believers? If so, why?

_____

_____

_____

_____

_____

What can you do to enrich the service?

_____

_____

_____

_____

_____

What is important to you in choosing a church home?

_____

_____

_____

Today's Prayer

Dear Lord Jesus, thank you for allowing me to see another day and giving me another opportunity to praise Your Holy name. Please keep me from growing weary in doing good. Let Your presence in me bless the people I join with in worship. Please help me to be more sensitive to your people. Let the gifts of Your Spirit develop in me and grow. Forgive me for times when I may have been self-centered and critical of your servants. Lead me to a church home where your Spirit is at work, and I can use my gifts. Thank you, Lord, in advance for your guidance. For those shut-in or unable to fellowship in person, guide them to sound teaching that their faith will not waver or they be deceived by false doctrine.

Thoughts

Group Study Questions

Has attending Church had an impact on you? If so, how?

Do you attend Church regularly? If so, why? If not, why?

What are the most important things to look for in choosing a church?

Day 17 - *About Faith*

Welcome to day 17! How would you say you are doing in the faith department? If you find yourself struggling with doubt, you are not alone. I think all of God's children have struggled with doubt at one time or another. Take a look at Peter, the Disciple of Jesus.

Matthew 14: 25-31 (NIV)

^{25} Shortly before dawn, Jesus went out to them, walking on the lake.

^{26} When the disciples saw him on the lake, they were terrified. "It's a ghost," they said, and cried out in fear.

^{27} But Jesus immediately said to them: "Take courage! It is I. Don't be afraid."

^{28} "Lord, if it's you," Peter replied, "tell me to come to you on the water."

^{29} "Come," he said. Then Peter got down out of the boat, walked on the water and came toward Jesus.

^{30} But when he saw the wind, he was afraid and, beginning to sink, cried out, "Lord, save me!"

^{31} Immediately, Jesus reached out his hand and caught him. "You of little faith," he said, "why did you doubt?"

Peter had been walking with Jesus for a while at this time. He had seen Jesus perform many miracles, and yet his faith wavered. Peter, like many of us, took his eyes off Jesus and focused on the storm. How many times have you and I done that? We start out with soaring faith; then, when we see adverse circumstances or listen to a nay-sayer, our faith goes out the window. It is imperative that we keep our focus on Jesus when we are in a storm.

Jesus is the source of our faith.

Hebrews 12:2 (NKJV)
[2] looking unto Jesus, the author and finisher of our faith, who for the joy that was set before Him endured the cross, despising the shame, and has sat down at the right hand of the throne of God.

The process for most people is they initially hear the Spoken Word; then, by His Spirit, the word resonates as truth in their inner being. They find themselves drawn to the truth as the Spirit of God speaks through the messenger to the person's inner being. Consequently, they believe what they are hearing. Once the seed of truth is planted, it begins to grow as it is cultivated. One of the main ways faith is developed is by often hearing the Spoken Word.

Romans 10:17 (NIV)
Consequently, faith comes by hearing, and hearing by the word of God.

Listening to a Bible app read to you is a great way to get familiar with the Bible. However, it is by no means a substitute for hearing the preached or taught word of God. Often, new believers will fall away from the faith because they attempt to learn the Bible on their own, and before long, they determine the Bible is too hard to understand, causing their interest to wane.

127

1 Corinthians 1:18 (NIV)
For the message of the cross is foolishness to those who are perishing, but to us who are being saved, it is the power of God.

Even those of you who have been a Christ follower for a long time will find that the Word of God is a living word; therefore, there is no time on this journey when the Word is irrelevant. Even a scripture you may have heard many times before may convey new revelation when the Holy Spirit speaks through His servant. As His Spirit is speaking, your faith is growing. Not sometimes...every time! You cannot be in the presence of God's spirit and not be affected even if you cannot feel any change at the moment. God's powerful Word changes you and equips you for the trials ahead.

In the following few lessons, I will share with you tools to help increase your faith, but first, let's see what the Bible says about faith.

Hebrews 11:1 (NKJV)
Now faith is the substance of things hoped for, the evidence of things not seen.

The Amplified version of the Bible reads Hebrews 11:1 this way:

Now faith is the assurance, (title deed, confirmation) of things hoped for (divinely guaranteed), and the evidence of things not seen [the conviction of the reality - faith comprehends as fact what cannot be experienced by physical senses].

128

Put another way, by faith, we are assured that what we hope for is a *done deal.* Faith, applied to our salvation, for example, means we have complete confidence that what the Bible says is true concerning our salvation.

Let's look at this example of salvation more closely.

Romans 10:9-10 (NIV)
[9] *If you declare with your mouth, "Jesus is Lord," and believe in your heart that God raised Him from the dead, you will be saved.*
[10] *For it is with your heart that you are justified, and it is with your mouth that you profess your faith and are saved.*

Following the act of repentance, when Romans 10:9 is actuated, you are saved and have eternal life! You are saved by faith. Simply believing and accepting that Jesus is Lord and died for your sins and was raised from the dead qualifies you to escape the penalty of sin (complete separation from God) and become a recipient of eternal life. See how powerful faith is? Faith is critical to our eternal life.

Faith is the evidence of things we cannot see. I liken this part of the verse to the wind. We cannot see the wind, yet we are absolutely sure and confident of its existence. We can feel the unseen force blowing against our faces. We witness the bending of trees, unable to resist the power that pushes against the tree's ability to stand. Objects are carried away by this invisible but present power. Not too different is faith in God's existence. We see the unmistakable works of His hands in our very being and in all the earth has to offer, yet a face-to-face encounter few have had.

The struggle with faith is different for different people. Some have no problem believing there is a God but may have trouble believing He sent His Son to earth to die to redeem us. Others believe in the redemption story but struggle with believing in God for answered prayer. No matter your struggle, there are ways to strengthen your faith. God is not mad at you because you struggle sometimes.

Mark 9: 14-26 (NIV)

[14] *And when He came to the disciples, He saw a great multitude around them, and scribes disputing with them.*

[15] *Immediately, when they saw him, all the people were greatly amazed, and running to Him, greeted Him.*

[16] *And He asked the scribes, "What are you discussing with them?"*

[17] *Then one of the crowd answered and said, "Teacher, I brought You, my son, who has a mute spirit.*

[18] *And whenever it seizes him, he throws him down; he foams at the mouth, gnashes his teeth, and becomes rigid. So, I spoke to Your disciples that they should cast it out, but they could not.*

[19] *He answered him and said, "O faithless generation, how long shall I be with you? How long shall I bear with you? Bring him to me.*

[20] *Then they brought him to him. And when he saw him, immediately the spirit convulsed him, and he fell on the ground and wallowed, foaming at the mouth.*

[21] *So He asked his father, " How long has this been happening to him?" And he said, "From childhood.*

²² And often he has thrown him both into the fire and into the water to destroy him. But if You can do anything, have compassion on us and help us."

²³ Jesus said to him, "If you can believe, all things are possible to him who believes."

*²⁴ Immediately, the father of the child cried out and said with tears, **"Lord, I believe; Help my unbelief!"***

²⁵ When Jesus saw that the people came running together, He rebuked the unclean spirit, saying to it "Deaf and dumb spirit, I command you, come out of him and enter him no more!"

²⁶ Then the spirit cried out, convulsed him greatly, and came out of him. And he became as one dead, so that many said, "He is dead." But Jesus took him by the hand and lifted him up, and he arose.

Notice the response of the man whose son was possessed. He was unsure of his own faith, and instead of trying to conceal his lack, he cried out to Jesus for help. Jesus's response was not to ridicule the man for lacking faith but to answer his prayer. Imagine how that man's ability to believe in God grew that day!

Our Lord is not a respecter of persons. If we are willing to call on Him for help, even if we need Him to strengthen our faith, He will surely answer. What looks impossible to us is an opportunity for God to show Himself and build our faith.

Today's Promise

Trust in the Lord, and do good; dwell in the land and befriend faithfulness. Delight yourself in the Lord, and he will give you the desires of your heart. Commit your way to the Lord's trust in him, and he will act.

Psalm 37:3-5

Study Questions

Why do you think the Lord said to the man, "If you believe."?

_____

_____

_____

_____

_____

What are you having trouble believing God for?

_____

_____

_____

_____

_____

What factors cause you to doubt?

_____

_____

_____

_____

_____

Today's Prayer

Dear Lord, there are times when it is difficult to hold on to my faith. Especially when it is something I have been praying about for a long time. Help me by the power of Your Spirit to be patient as I wait for answered prayer to manifest. Help my faith in You to grow stronger. Forgive me when I waver in trusting you with every aspect of my life.

Thoughts

_____

_____

_____

_____

_____

Group Study

2 Corinthians 5:7: "We walk by faith, and not by sight."

Share what you find challenging in your walk of faith.

What does 'Walk by faith and not by sight' mean?

Day 18 - *Faith Building Tools*

Welcome back! Have you ever desired to have more faith? In the last lesson, we are reminded of God's willingness to answer prayer. We discussed how simply asking God to increase your faith is undoubtedly helpful. But what about the times when it seems God is not responding? Have you ever experienced - amid a hard situation – that though you pray earnestly or cry out to the Lord, there seems to be no relief? Again, you are not alone.

Psalm 77:1-2 (NIV)
[1] *I cried out to God for help; I cried out to God to hear me.*
[2] *When I was in distress, I sought the Lord; at night, I stretched out my tiring hands, and I would not be comforted.*

The psalmist is praying earnestly, crying out to the Lord in anguish. His hands are stretched out in prayer, but it seems his prayers are not being answered.

"And I would not be comforted."

Other translations, closer to the writer's original intent, say, "My soul refused to be comforted". The psalmist resisted all suggestions that came into his mind that might bring comfort. His heart was melancholy and downcast, his spirit crushed, and his mind in such a negative place that he chose to dwell only on his dark thoughts. As he embraced gloomy, sad thoughts, it filled his soul, leaving no room for any thoughts of consolation or peace. Overwhelmed.

Psalm 77:3-4 (NIV)

³ *I remembered you, God, and I groaned; I meditated, and my spirit grew faint.*

⁴ *You kept my eyes from closing; I was too troubled to speak.*

The psalmist thinks of God but is now so exhausted his spirit is weakening. The condition that so deeply troubles him has caused so much distress he cannot sleep or even speak any words. He has found himself reduced to groaning. Have you ever found yourself in this condition? I have.

Let me stop here for a moment.

For anyone reading this who is going through a very difficult time, whether it be betrayal, pain, sickness, financial calamity, loss of a loved one, a loved one addicted to substance or even loneliness, or any one of life's challenging trials or tribulations, I pray for you as I am writing this. I pray that the Holy Spirit will meet you where you are. That He will give you peace through the storm. That He will meet your every need. That you will feel His great love for you! I pray, Lord Jesus, that You will heal any broken heart reading this and bring comfort. Lord, supernaturally, send your Spirit to help in this time of crisis for the person reading this right now! Restore, refresh, and grant them a larger portion of faith. Help them come through this trial victoriously and with a testimony! Through this experience, impart a greater understanding of who You are. In Jesus name! I give You all praise! Honor! And Glory! I believe, on their behalf, that it is done! Amen

Relief is on the way! Praise His Holy Name in faith! Expect it!

Now, back to the psalmist. So, let's see what the psalmist does next:

Psalm 77: 5-9 (NIV)

[5] I thought about the former days, the years of long ago;

[6] I remembered my songs in the night. My heart meditated, and my spirit asked:

[7] "Will the Lord reject forever? Will he never show his favor again?

[8] Has his unfailing love vanished forever? Has his promise failed for all time?

[9] Has God forgotten to be merciful? Has he in anger withheld his compassion?"

The psalmist forces himself to reflect on the things regarding God in the past, how God delivered His people from Egypt, and many more challenging situations. God's record demonstrated His unfailing faithfulness.

1. **Faith Building Tool:**

   When the future seems too daunting, turn to what God has done for others when they found themselves in formidable circumstances. Many accounts of God stepping in to rescue His people can be found in the scriptures.

The songwriter Jim Reeves wrote in the infamous hymn: 'There is no Secret What God Can Do,' 'What He has done for others, He can do for you,"... which leads right to the following tool.

136

The psalmist began to think of songs that had brought comfort in the past. Songs of thanksgiving rather than cries of sorrow. Songs he used to sing at night before bed.

2. **Faith Building Tool:**

   Sometimes, the words of praise and worship songs can lift your spirit and strengthen your faith. Many praise and worship songs are anointed *(having the ability to draw us closer to God through worship)*. Having the right kinds of songs in your memory bank is crucial so the Holy Spirit can pull them up in time of need.

The psalmist began to consider what he knew of God's character and track record, which can be found in the scriptures. God's record shows He has always been forgiving, always shown favor, always had unfailing love, always kept His promises, and always been merciful. By thinking about these things, the goodness of God, the direction of his thoughts began to change. 'Is it possible that God was so angry that He was no longer compassionate?' the psalmist contemplated.

Finally, the psalmist concludes:

Psalm 77:10 (NIV)
And I said, This is my anguish: but I will remember the years of the right hand of the most High.

Here, we see the psalmist begin to take a turn. After thoughtful reflection, he decides that whatever his personal condition or the current condition of God's people, God is still who He said He is—the years of ages past presented too

137

compelling an argument in defense of God's unfailing and unchanging character.

God is sovereign. There are many times when there will be no immediate answers that can explain the mind of God. Why God allows circumstances that seem contrary to our well-being is a question most have pondered at one time or another.

The psalmist wisely resolves that it is his own weakness that has caused him to call God's character into question. His thoughts are now back on the right track; as he ponders the goodness of God, he realizes that even without an explanation as to why things are so bad, he cannot dismiss what he has already learned about God. He decides to accept or *to know that he doesn't know*. Understanding that, unlike God, he is finite in his thinking, he resolves to hold on to what he does know… that **God is unchanging and worthy of our trust.**

Psalm 77: 11-12 (NIV)
[11] *I will remember the deeds of the LORD: yes, I will remember your miracles of long ago.*
[12] *I will consider all of your works and meditate on all your mighty deeds.*

Remembering what God has already done is one of the main ways to help build faith, especially in times of trouble. Biblically, we are encouraged to rehearse or remind ourselves of His past miracles. The psalmist reminds himself of the miracles in Israel's past—God's faithfulness to His chosen people, the Israelites.

The Israelites shared an extraordinary relationship with God. God said, "They will be my people, and I will be their God."

138

Here's the great news... this includes you! As a believer and follower of Christ, you are now included as one of His chosen people. God's faithfulness, mercy, grace, and Love apply as much to you as to the Israelites, Hebrews, or Jews! (*Different names, same people*) You were grafted into the family of God when you received Christ as your Lord and Savior. Whether born a Jew or Gentile, you are now an heir to the kingdom of the Most High God! Therefore, the very faith-building miracles that the psalmist reflected on, you can also. The same favor God showed to those in the Old Testament, you can share the same expectations.

3. **Faith Building Tool:**

    Journal. Keep an account of your experiences with God. One of our human flaws is quickly forgetting about a problem once we no longer have it. I liken it to a headache. How often do you remember the headache once it has passed? If you do not keep a journal, consider keeping one. This will allow you to look back at your history with God. You will see His faithfulness in your life, as many of the prayers you penned to paper will have been answered when you look back. This not only builds faith but also your testimony.

Remembering your encounters with God strengthens your faith by leaps and bounds. No longer is it about what God has done for someone else, but what God has done for you.

Today's Promise

Do not be anxious about anything, but in everything, by prayer and supplication with thanksgiving let your requests be made known to God. And the peace of God, which surpasses all understanding, will guard your hearts and your minds in Christ Jesus.

Philippians 4:6-7

Study Questions

How about your past? Are there miracles in your history? Write down several that you can remember.

_____

_____

_____

_____

_____

Can you remember an impossible situation that God brought you through?

_____

_____

_____

_____

_____

What impact did the circumstance have on your faith while in the situation?

_____

_____

_____

_____

_____

How was your faith impacted after God intervened?

_____

_____

_____

_____

_____

Today's Prayer

Oh, Holy, Heavenly Father. Thank you for all you have done and are doing. Thank you for your unfailing Love. I acknowledge that You are in control of all things. Lord, there is so much going on in my life and this world that I don't understand. I often get discouraged and overwhelmed when I look at so many things going wrong and have no way to fix them. I know You have promised to hear our prayers and answer them. You promise to take care of our needs, but from my vantage point, things look pretty grim. By your Spirit, remind me how you have been faithful to me all my life when I struggle with my faith. Let songs of Thanksgiving come to my mind. I desire to meditate on Your goodness. Help me to stop negative thoughts from running around in my head. Again, on This day, I ask you to provide me with an increase of faith, not just me but increase the faith of all your children who are struggling in these last and evil days. Thank you for Your grace that covers us in our weakness. Amen

Thoughts

_____

_____

_____

_____

_____

Group Study Questions

Share what stories in the Bible have encouraged you in the past.

Share a song with the group that has lifted your spirit in a time of discouragement.

Discuss what is a source of faith for you.

Go the Lord together in prayer and ask Him to increase the faith in all of you.

Day 19 - *Faith in Action*

By this point in this study, it is understood that salvation is based on faith – not works. We cannot 'good deed' ourselves into heaven. Eternal life is based on our belief in the work done on the cross by Jesus Christ. So, is that all there is to it? Have you ever asked why so many people who identify as Christians are so comfortable living a sinful lifestyle? Is it possible to believe that Jesus Christ is Lord – just not your Lord?

> ### *James 2:14 (NKJV)*
> *What does it profit, my brethren, if someone **says** he has faith but does not have works? Can Faith save him?*

It has been a contention for some that James 2:14 is contradicting what Paul in Ephesians 2:8-9

> ### *Ephesians 2:8-9 (NKJV)*
> [8] *"For it is by grace you have been saved, through faith -and this is not from yourselves, it is the gift of God,*
> [9] *not of works, should any man boast.*

James is not contradicting Paul, as it may appear if not examined closely. James is addressing the abuse of grace that was becoming prevalent among believers – not so different from today. James was challenging believers to study their behavior. Is your life a reflection of what you *say* you believe? If Jesus is your Lord, wouldn't you obey Him?

Many profess faith, but is it true faith? The operative word in James 2:14 is "**says**" he has faith. This implies that some say they believe but do not honestly believe. It is not good works that are a condition of salvation but faith that Jesus is the Christ who died for your sins and rose on the third day; however, *true* faith brings about transformation. This is not to say that once you believe you are suddenly bound by the law, that is not the case; however, if you believe that Jesus is Lord but not just Lord but your Lord, then a desire to not purposely offend Him by continuing in sinful behavior should naturally follow. One should be inspired to obey Him -- following His example and learning all there is to know about living a life pleasing to God *if* He is your God.

James 2:15-17 (NKJV)
[15] *If a brother or sister is naked and destitute of daily food,*
[16] *and one of you says to them, "Depart in peace, be warmed, and filled," but you do not give them the things which are needed for the body, what does it profit?*
[17] *Thus also faith by itself; if it does not have works, it's dead.*

James 2:15-17 gives us a practical example of how useless words are if not followed up with deeds. Faith is designed to produce good works. Faith is intended to lead to a Holy life. It is questionable how genuine faith is; that has no evidence.

James 2:18-19 (NKJV)
[18] *But someone will say, "You have faith, and I have works. "Show me your faith without works, and I will show you my faith **by** my works.*
[19] *You believe that there is one God. You do well. Even the demons believe - and tremble!*

What does faith without works look like? Nothing! There is nothing to see—only words lost in the wind... without evidence of existence. Rather than someone talking about how great their faith is, James's faith is evident by how he lives, his choices, and how he conducts himself. The works James does is because he has faith. There is no doubt of his justification because there is evidence of his faith, which is his works.

Driving the point home, James points out that even demons believe and fear God. Demons are fully aware there is one true God, but that is not the God they serve. Needless to say, they are still hell bound. Hence, just declaring that there is one God is not doing much more than demons.

James 2:20-26 (NKJV)
20 *But do you want to know, O foolish man, that faith without works is dead?*
21 *Was not Abraham our father justified by works when he offered Isaac his son on the altar?*
22 *Do you see that faith was working together with his works, and by works, faith was made perfect?*
23 *And the scripture was fulfilled which says, "Abraham believed God, and it was accounted to him for righteousness." And he was called the friend of God.*
24 *You see, then that man is justified by works, and not by faith only.*
25 *Likewise, was not Rahab the harlot also justified by words when. She received the messengers and sent them out another way?*
26 *For as the body without the spirit is dead, so faith without works is dead also.*

James emphasizes his argument in verse 20 that it is foolish to argue that there can be faith without works. He cites

Abraham as an example of being justified by the action he took because of his faith. Action completes faith. Put another way, for faith to be perfect, it must be coupled with or accompanied by action.

Rahab believed that the God of Israel was the true God and with his people, so she hid the spies and protected them. She was saved and justified by the action she took. Her belief produced action - action that was pleasing to God.

There is a lot of emphasis put on grace in the New Testament. This comes on the heels of Judaism, a religion that was so rigorous, with its 613 laws, that it had become a weight and a burden on those attempting to uphold them. The law only reveals our inability to keep the law. By the time Jesus came to earth, many people practicing religious rituals had lost complete sight of God. After Christ, the 'golden law' became the law capsulized in two commandments by the words of Jesus Christ.

Mark 12: 29-31 (NKJV)
²⁹ *Jesus answered, "The first of all the commandments is 'Hear, O Israel, the Lord our God, the Lord is one.*
³⁰ *And you shall love the Lord your God with all your heart, with all your soul, with all your mind, and with all your strength.' This is the first commandment.*
³¹ *And the second, like it, is this: 'You shall love your neighbor as yourself.' There is no greater commandment greater than these.*

With the burden of the law lifted and grace being introduced, some have taken grace for granted, causing a shadow of doubt on their faith. Their behavior is no different from a non-believer. Freedom in Christ is not a license to say and do anything you want and claim Jesus already paid for my sins, so I'm fine. I urge you not to ignore the prompting of the Holy Spirit or the conviction of the Spirit. If you allow His Holy Spirit to lead you, you will know what grieves the spirit and what pleases Him.

In conclusion of today, if being a Christian was a crime, would there be enough evidence against you to be convicted? Would the way you live, your attitude, your response to conflict, your care for others, your generosity, your quickness to forgive, or your kindness give you away?

Today's Promise

Therefore, confess your sins to each other and pray for each other so that you may be healed. The prayer of a righteous person is powerful and effective.

James 5:16

Study Questions

How does your faith manifest? What are works that identify you as a Christ follower?

_____

_____

_____

_____

_____

What changes have you seen in your life since your salvation?

_____

_____

_____

_____

_____

How is faith exercised in repentance?

_____

_____

_____

_____

Today's prayer

Dear Lord. Let my life be a living testimony of my faith in you. I want to live so that You can be seen in me. Help me to yield to your Spirit. Let me vanish, and you come through. Forgive me for the times I've been flippant about my walk, taking grace for granted. Amen

Thoughts

_____

_____

_____

_____

Group Study Questions

Share a time when your faith has been called into question.

How can ungodly behavior from a Christian impact their testimony?

What are the 'works' James is talking about? Give examples.

Day 20 - *Last Days*

Welcome to Day 20. You have made it to just about the end of this study. We are living in the final days of prophecy. Our Lord is coming back soon. Each day that passes, more prophesies spoken of in the Bible are being realized. Today, we will explore what Jesus Christ revealed about the 7 Churches in the end times.

Some theologians will argue that these letters to particular churches are symbolic, while others believe the messages were specific only to each church mentioned, having no bearing on today's church. Rather than engage in such a debate, I am going to consider the word to be addressing all of those reading what was being said to the Churches since after each letter to the 7 churches, He repeats the phrase *"He who has an ear let him hear what the Spirit says to the churches."* This tells me, to all those reading these letters, *Listen Up!*

Are many Churches today a reflection of the seven churches named in Revelations? Today, we will look in-depth at the first four churches named in Revelations chapter 2 and see if there are recognizable similarities in churches today.

While we do this lesson and look at the church as a group, please keep in mind that we, Christ's followers, are the church. So, while we are looking at the church as a group of people, I strongly encourage you to look at what is being said to the seven churches as a personal word also and, if applicable, warnings. These latter-day churches include us. Whether or not we identify with the name or region mentioned, we are the church's people right now! As we probe into each letter, it would be wise to examine yourself.

150

Let's be sure we are not committing any of the offenses mentioned in these letters.

First Church: Ephesus
Revelations 2:1-3 (NIV)
[1] *"To the angel of the church of Ephesus write, 'These things says He who holds the seven stars in His right hand, who walks in the midst of the seven golden lampstands:*
[2] *"I know your works, your labor, your patience, and that you cannot bear those who are evil. And you have tested those who say they are apostles and are not, and have found them liars;* [3] *and you have persevered and have patience, and have labored for My name's sake and have not become weary.*

Though the Church of Ephesus had done many things right, such as working diligently, not growing weary, not allowing evil to infiltrate the church, and testing those who claimed to be apostles but were, in fact, liars, there was still a grievance the Lord had with them.

Revelation 2:4-6 (NIV)
[4] *Nevertheless, I have this against you, that you have left your first love.*
[5] *Remember therefore from where you have fallen; repent and do the first works, or else I will come to you quickly and remove your lampstand from its place—unless you repent.*
[6] *But this you have, that you hate the deeds of the Nicolaitans, which I also hate.*

The first love here inferred is the zealousness and enthusiasm they had at the beginning of their walk with

Christ. This is not uncommon in relationships. People start in a new relationship with much excitement; then, over time, people begin to take one another for granted. They no longer do the things for each other they started out doing when they were in love.

Do you remember when you couldn't wait for the church doors to open...when the highlight of your week was Sunday service and mid-week Bible study? Many people, like the church of Ephesus, slowly lost the passion for God they once had. Yes, they are still diligently working, but the flame of love for Jesus is almost out.

Here is an example:

When you were first saved and excited about your faith, did you not invite others to church and witness often? When was the last time you shared your faith? Maybe you were one to give generously to the Church or help anywhere that was needed. Has that changed or fallen off? Become less important? Perhaps you once had a particular time and place where you met with the Lord daily but now rarely find the time.

Regaining the beginning passion once it has dwindled is not so easy. If you have found yourself in this state, you are urged to remember where you once were, repent, and begin doing what you initially did.

Revelations 2:7 (NIV)
"He who has an ear, let him hear what the Spirit says to the churches. *To him who overcomes I will give to eat from the tree of life, which is in the midst of the Paradise of God."*

There is a promise of eternal life to those who heed this warning. Tree of Life! Restored to the state of relationship with God that Adam and Eve before the fall! Let's overcome! If you are reading this, there is still time to correct it. Thank God for His grace. It is so easy to drift away- unnoticed- but God, in His infinite grace, finds a way to reach us.

Second Church: Smyrna
Revelations 2:8-10 (NIV)
> [8] *"And to the angel of the church in Smyrna write, 'These things say the First and the Last, who was dead, and came to life:*
> [9] *"I know your works, tribulation, and poverty (but you are rich); and I know the blasphemy of those who say they are Jews and are not, but are a synagogue of Satan.*
> [10] *Do not fear any of those things which you are about to suffer. Indeed, the devil is about to throw some of you into prison, that you may be tested, and you will have tribulation ten days. Be faithful until death, and I will give you the crown of life.*

This branch of the church dealt with great poverty and persecution. They were tasked to endure great suffering. In the United States of America, this level of persecution has not yet reached our shores, though there is no doubt it is coming. Many Christians worldwide are enduring this type of persecution and have been for decades. For those of you in these circumstances, it will be only a short time compared to eternity. Ten days represent a short time, and you will be delivered. Though you die, yet shall you live! Jesus promises you a crown of life.

Revelations 2:11 (NIV)
"He who has an ear, let him hear what the
Spirit says to the churches. *He who overcomes*
shall not be hurt by the second death. "

Are you prepared to defend your faith if it means facing prison or death? This is a real test of faith for many of our brothers and sisters worldwide. By the power of His Holy Spirit, many overcome and pay the ultimate cost. Praise be to our Lord, who strengthens us in our darkest hour!

Third Church: Pergamos
Revelations 2:12-13 (NIV)
[12] *And to the angel of the church in Pergamos write, 'These things says He who has the sharp two-edged sword:*
[13] *I know now your works, and where you dwell, where Satan's throne is. And you hold fast to My name and did not deny My faith even in the days in which Antipas was My faithful martyr, who was killed among you, where Satan dwells.'*

Pergamos was located in the capital city of the Roman province of Asia Minor. The persecution against the church was great, as was the pressure to conform to the wicked culture. The governor of that Roman Province had the authority to choose which prisoners would live and which would die - known as the 'The Right of the Sword'. Being accused of not honoring the so-called 'divine' Caesar was enough to get a person killed.

This city, Pergamum, was the first city to institute the cult of emperor worship. Caesar Augustus, the Roman emperor, was not only worshiped at the Athena temple but was declared divine and claimed to be their god and king.

Jesus reminds them (*and us*) that He is the ultimate authority on life and death. The Lord acknowledges how difficult living in such a wicked place is.

Revelations 2:14-16 (NIV)

[14] *But I have a few things against you, because you have there, those who hold the doctrine of Balaam, who taught Balak to put a stumbling block before the children of Israel, to eat things sacrificed to idols, and to commit sexual immorality.*

[15] *Thus, you also have those who hold the doctrine of the Nicolaitans, which thing I hate.*

[16] *Repent, or else I will come to you quickly and will fight against them with the sword of My mouth.*

So, what was the doctrine of Balaam?

Balac, the king of Moab, feared the Israelites who were on the brink of crossing the Jordon River into the land of promise, so he sought out Balaam, a prophet, so that through this renowned prophet, he might curse God's people.

Although unable to curse God's people, Balaam eventually caused them to error. (sin) All this was done for material gain. When enough money was involved, Balaam compromised his loyalty—often called the prophet for profit.

Many Christians have been drawn into using the church as a self-profiting tool. The word 'Pergamos' relates to bigamy and polygamy. Israel mixed with the Moab women, part of Balaam's wicked scheme, to lead Israel into sin: mixed marriage. Marriage of the church (God's people) and the world. How many of God's people have exchanged Godly integrity for profit?

God and money – can't serve both.

Revelations 2:17 (NIV)
"He who has an ear, let him hear what the
Spirit says to the churches. To him who
overcomes I will give some of the hidden manna
to eat. And I will give him a white stone, and on
the stone, a new name written which no one
knows except him who receives it."

Fourth Church: Thyatira
Revelations 2:18-20 (NIV)
[18] *And to the angel of the church in Thyatira*
write, 'These things says the Son of God, who has
eyes like a flame of fire, and His feet like fine
brass:

Eyes that see and expose everything. Feet capable of crushing nations.

[19] *"I know your works, love, service, faith, and*
your patience; and as for your works, the
last are more than the first.

It is quite an accomplishment that this church was/is doing more in the end than in the beginning. Often, people start with a bang but dwindle towards the end. 'Grow weary of doing good.

156

20 Nevertheless, I have a few things against you because you allow that woman Jezebel, who calls herself a prophetess, to teach and seduce My servants to commit sexual immorality and eat things sacrificed to idols.

This woman, called Jezebel, seduced people in the church to commit fornication. It is implied, though not affirmed, that she practiced what she taught.

This particular grievance is all too often found in churches today. I have witnessed people being put in leadership positions in the church who had no business in a place of influence. Usually, the elevated title is tied to how much they give to the church. In many cases, one would question whether or not they were even believers. Often, they certainly did not believe the Bible to be the inspired Word of God and therefore taught compromising views. I am sad to say I cannot count how many people who consider themselves 'Christians' taught their children that fornication is 'okay.' That the Bible is out of touch with the changing culture and sex outside of marriage is no big deal... it's a natural act between consenting parties.

One woman, for instance, an ordained minister in the church, was allowed to start a woman's class. By the end of the course, over fifty percent of the women who attended her class had come to believe they were no longer happy with their spouses and filed for divorce. It was unbelievable how many families were torn apart. After she had done much damage (*the adversary's mission accomplished*), this minister left the state - but not alone. She ran off with another minister's wife. The pastor was warned about this woman's influence, but the warnings were brushed aside.

157

As for meat offered to idols, usually, partaking in meat offered to idols required the person to attend idol worshiping ceremonies. These ceremonies typically included overindulgence of wine and consuming raw/rare bloody meat, followed by wild, lewd, promiscuous behavior. At these festivals, unlimited toleration for indulgence in sexual immorality took place.

What might the Church of Thyatira look like in today's culture? Reminded me of Mardi Gras on Bourbon St., New Orleans. Put on a mask, and anything goes. People drinking alcohol until they vomit on the streets, compromised judgment, women and men exposing themselves... does this sound familiar? A woman I knew attended a church where Mardi Gras festival attendance was an annual church excursion. Those who participated joked about what happens in New Orleans - stays in New Orleans. The exact phrase is used for Las Vegas - otherwise known as Sin City. The Lord reminds us He sees it all. Nothing is hidden from Him.

Revelations 2:21-22 (NIV)
21 And I gave her time to repent of her sexual immorality, and she did not repent.
22 Indeed, I will cast her into a sickbed, and those who commit adultery with her into great tribulation, unless they repent of their deeds.

Here again, we see God's far-reaching grace. God is known for giving people plenty of time and chances to change their wicked ways.

Revelations 2:23-25 (NIV)
23 I will kill her children with death, and all the churches shall know that I am He who searches

158

*the minds and hearts. And I will give to each one
of you according to your works.*
²⁴ *"Now to you I say, and to the rest in Thyatira,
as many as do not have this doctrine, who have
not known the depths of Satan, as they say, I will
put on you no other burden.*
²⁵ *But hold fast what you have till I come.*

What I will coin as **'The Doctrine of Permissiveness'**
spoken of in verse 24, an insensitive and dismissive doctrine
about God's position on sin and encourages sinful behavior,
is satanic! This doctrine of taking sin lightly and grace for
granted is very dangerous. To take grace for granted means
to underestimate the value of grace or treat it with contempt.

Hebrews 10:26-31 (NIV)
²⁶ *For if we sin willfully after we have received
the knowledge of the truth, there no longer
remains a sacrifice for sins*
²⁷ *but a certain fearful expectation of judgment,
and fiery indignation which will devour the
adversaries.*
²⁸ *Anyone who has rejected Moses' law dies
without mercy on the testimony of two or three
witnesses*
²⁹ *of how much worse punishment, do you
suppose, will he be thought worthy who has
trampled the Son of God underfoot, counted the
blood of the covenant by which he was
sacrificed, a common thing, and insulted the
Spirit of grace?*
³⁰ *For we know Him who said, "Vengeance is
mine, I will repay," says the Lord. And again,
"The Lord will judge His people."*

159

³¹ *It is a fearful thing to fall into the hands of the living God.*

Today's Promise

And he who overcomes, and keeps My works until the end, to him I will give power over the nations— 'He shall rule them with a rod of iron: They shall be dashed to pieces like the potter's vessels' – as I also have received from My Father, and I will give him the morning star.

Revelations 2:26-28

Revelations 2:29 (NIV)
"He who has an ear, let him hear what the Spirit says to the churches."

Bible Study Questions

Think back to the things you did when you were first saved. Have you lost your zeal? If so, what should you do?

_____

_____

_____

_____

_____

Are you in a tribulation or a trial that threatens your life or livelihood? Are you enduring persecution as a result of your faith? If so, how are you coping?

_____

_____

_____

_____

_____

Does the church you attend talk about the consequences of sin or only God's love and grace?

_____

_____

Does money seem to be a big influencer in your church? Is potential money opportunity part of your motivation for what you do 'for the Lord'?

_____

_____

Is Godly behavior encouraged, or is the influence of the world and its views prevalent in your church?

_____

_____

Today's Prayer

Wow, Lord, thank you for showing me areas to be aware of in these last days. Help me not to stumble and get caught up in anything that grieves you. Use me to be an example of a follower of yours. Please give me the wisdom and discernment to recognize false and dangerous doctrines. Restore the joy of my salvation. Forgive me if I have neglected our relationship in any way. Oh, how I love You! Thank you for this day. Fill me fresh with your Spirit and guide my every move.

Thoughts

_____

_____

_____

_____

_____

Group Study Questions

What should you do if you notice negative characteristics of any of the four churches discussed today in your church?

How would you handle a person in leadership who teaches nonbiblical principles if it were in your church?

Should you leave the church when you see problems similar to the four churches in your Church?

Did Jesus tell those who were not caught up in the sin prevalent in the church but were standing fast and faithful to leave the church?

Day 21 - *Last Day*

Congratulations! You made it to the final day! If you have been a Christian for a while, I'm sure you have heard that these are the last days – that the second coming of Christ is due any day now. I have been preaching 'He is coming soon' for over 45 years. At sixteen, I thought the world couldn't get any more wicked. Oh - how wrong I was!

Nonetheless, I was convinced the time was up for this world. I am still persuaded that time is short, but who knows precisely what short is to God? Another 50 years is not a long time considering the age of the world, but enough time for many people to die without seeing the rapture. What I am convinced of is you never know when He is coming for you. Even if the world continues for another 100 years, are you ready to meet Him if He comes for you in the next 10 minutes?

The last three letters to the churches are our final topic. It is an excellent opportunity to compare your standard of Christianity with God's expectations of the church as a whole and you as an individual.

Fifth Church: Sardis
Revelations 3:1 (NIV)
To the angel of the church in Sardis write: These are the words of him who holds the seven spirits of God and the seven stars. I know your deeds; you have a reputation of being alive, but you are dead.

It is easy for people to gain the reputation of being a Christian, even participate in doing good deeds; however,

163

here we see that a person can appear to be a spirit-led Christ follower and not be in Christ at all. Apart from Christ, we are no more than a withered branch fit to be burned.

John 15:6 (NIV)
I am the vine; you are the branches. If you remain in me and I in you, you will bear much fruit; apart from me you can do nothing. If you do not remain in me, you are like a branch that is thrown away and withers; such branches are picked up, thrown into the fire and burned.

Have you ever attended a church where everyone seems excited about doing good work? Maybe they do lots of charity and various community programs, but their work doesn't result in any change in their lives or others. They start a work, like ministering through a community event, but never finish the work by following up with those they contacted. What about churches that have people respond to the alter call, but no one follows up on the new convert? No one even notices if the recent convert is ever seen again. If you had an employee who starts a job but has yet to finish what they have begun, what would you do with that employee?

We can fall into the same sin of the church in Sardis if we are not careful—Gung ho initially but unreliable and inconsistent long term. The lack of consistent faithfulness in our walk grieves the Spirit of God. When we are inconsistent, it also affects our testimony. Have you ever met someone who volunteers for everything and follows up on nothing? What opinion, over time, do you form about such a person?

Many say "I love the Lord" loud and often, but when it comes time to obey Him, even the simple things He has asked of His people are often neglected or half-done. Someone in this state may (for example) attend service occasionally or perhaps come every week but manage to be late enough to miss praise, worship, and even parts of the message.

A side note: An immature or weak Christian may behave similarly to an insincere or non-Christian. So, let's be careful not to judge. We are unable to tell the tares from the wheat. The enemy does all he can to distract and occupy God's people's time so they don't find a minute to spend with God to hear His voice. This enemy tactic has been an ongoing trial for God's people. Television, the internet, social media, music, phones (with all that entails), and even church work can get in the way of staying connected to Jesus, the vine, and our life source.

Revelations 3:2 (NIV)
Wake up! Strengthen what remains and is about to die, for I have found your deeds unfinished in the sight of my God. Remember, therefore, what you have received and heard; hold it fast and repent. But if you do not wake up, I will come like a thief, and you will not know at what time I will come to you.

What a profound warning! 'Wake up' indicates too many of us are asleep - not living as though we take His coming or our job as a servant of the Lord seriously. Think about this: would you be ready if He were to come as a thief in the night for you? There will be no time or opportunity to get it right. Time out! Game over! Will He find a plow in your hand? Or

165

will He find you caught up in all types of distractions? Is your relationship with the Lord on the back burner?

Look very carefully at your state and examine yourself. Ask the Gracious Lord to show you where you may be in error. If any of what is being said in this letter to the church of Sardis applies to you, take action.

- Remember the joy of your salvation. Reflect on what you were taught at the beginning of your walk with God.
- Grab hold of the things that you can still identify. Good desires, Godly influences—time in prayer and the word.
- Repent. Humble yourself before the Lord. He is quick to forgive.

I pray for those reading this that the Holy Spirit quickens your spirit with a sense of urgency to get busy and consistent in your walk. For those holding on, I pray the Lord Jesus strengthens you to remain faithful to your call until He comes for the church or you individually.

Yet you have a few people in Sardis who have not soiled their clothes. They will walk with me, dressed in white, for they are worthy. The one who is victorious will, like them, be dressed in white. I will never blot out the name of that person from the Book of Life, but will acknowledge that name before my Father and His angels.

The thought of God's ability to blot out a name from the Book of Life is sobering.

Revelations 3:6 (NIV)
"He who has an ear, let him hear what the
Spirit says to the churches."

Sixth Church: Philadelphia
Revelations 3:7-9 (NIV)
7 *To the angel of the church in Philadelphia*
write: These are the words of him who is holy and
true, who holds the key of David. What he opens,
no one can shut, and what he shuts, no one can
open.
8 *I know your deeds. See, I have placed before*
you an open door that no one can shut. I know
that you have little strength, yet you have kept my
word and have not denied my name.
9 *I will make those who are of the synagogue of*
Satan, who claim to be Jews though they are not,
but are liars—I will make them come and fall
down at your feet and acknowledge that I have
loved you.

To those who remain faithful and true to the faith, who have
not succumbed to the pressure of this world to deny Christ.
Jesus, the holy and true one, has placed an open door before
them! An entry in which He holds the key! In these last and
evil days, the Lord has opened a door and made a way for
the faithful to bring forth the Gospel - withstanding great
opposition from the enemy.

Revelations 3:10 (NIV)
Since you have kept my command to endure
patiently, I will also keep you from the hour of
trial that is going to come on the whole world to
test the inhabitants of the earth.

There is coming a time of great tribulation upon the people of the earth, but our Lord says He will spare those who have remained faithful. Though there is much debate as to the meaning of this scripture. I have no doubt this passage references the promised rapture soon to come. The rapture is an event prophesied in the Bible that says the Lord will come and remove His people before the worst of the worst that will happen to the inhabitants of the earth.

Matthew 24:36-44 (NIV)

[36] But about that day or hour, no one knows, not even the angels in heaven, nor the Son, but only the Father.

[37] As it was in the days of Noah, so it will be at the coming of the Son of Man.

[38]For in the days before the flood, people were eating and drinking, marrying and giving in marriage, up to the day Noah entered the ark;

[39] and they knew nothing about what would happen until the flood came and took them all away. That is how it will be at the coming of the Son of Man.

[40] Two men will be in the field; one will be taken and the other left.

[41] Two women will be grinding with a hand mill; one will be taken and the other left.

[42] Therefore, keep watch, because you do not know on what day your Lord will come.

[43] But understand this: If the owner of the house had known at what time of night the thief was coming, he would have kept watch and would not have let his house be broken into.

168

⁴⁴ *So, you also must be ready, because the Son of Man will come at an hour when you do not expect him.*

Revelations 3:11-12 (NIV)

¹¹ *I am coming soon. Hold on to what you have so that no one will take your crown.*
¹² *The one who is victorious, I will make a pillar in the temple of my God. Never again will they leave it. I will write on them the name of my God and the name of the city of my God, the new Jerusalem, which is coming down out of heaven from my God; and I will also write on them my new name.*

1 Thessalonians 4:16-17 (NIV)

¹⁶ *For the Lord himself will come down from heaven, with a loud command, with the voice of the archangel and with the trumpet call of God, and the dead in Christ will rise first.*
¹⁷ *After that, we who are still alive and are left will be caught up together with them in the clouds to meet the Lord in the air. And so we will be with the Lord forever. Therefore encourage one another with these words.*

Revelations 3:13 (NIV)

"He who has an ear, let him hear what the Spirit says to the churches."

Seventh Church: Laodicea
Revelations 3:14-18 (NIV)

¹⁴ *To the angel of the church in Laodicea, write: These are the words of the Amen, the faithful and true witness, the ruler of God's creation.*

¹⁵ *I know your deeds, that you are neither cold nor hot. I wish you were either one or the other!*
¹⁶ *So, because you are lukewarm—neither hot nor cold—I am about to spit you out of my mouth.*
¹⁷ *You say, 'I am rich; I have acquired wealth and do not need a thing.' But you do not realize that you are wretched, pitiful, poor, blind and naked.*
¹⁸ *I counsel you to buy from me gold refined in the fire, so you can become rich; and white clothes to wear, so you can cover your shameful nakedness; and salve to put on your eyes, so you can see.*

Neither hot nor cold. Not fervent regarding Jesus nor oblivious to Jesus, but lukewarm is the state of this church. If the church were zealous for Christ, that would be definitive where they stand, or if they knew nothing of Christ, then maybe they could be reached and redeemed. Instead, they straddle the fence. Neither all in or all out. For this reason, Jesus says He will cast them from His presence unless they repent.

I once was asked by a young woman why so many Christians were not wealthy. I thought about this and concluded that there are many wealthy Christians. They work hard and are prosperous. Yet many others live lives depending on God for everything.

God says He owns a thousand cattle upon a thousand hills. In other words, there is no end to the supply of riches He has at his disposal. So why doesn't He fill our accounts with money? It would be an easy miracle for Him.

170

At the time of this encounter, I had two children in college. I thought about them. What if I, too, had riches galore? Would I stock their bank account so they had no needs? My answer was 'No'. Why? Because I know that being the young age they were, that would be the last time I would hear from them until the money ran out or they destroyed themselves with it. Our relationship would be stalled from growing as they would be too busy with the world to check in with parents. My relationship with them and my ability to guide them in the early years of adulthood was too important to lose. If they, like many of us, no longer see the need for authority or guidance in their lives, good luck with getting them to check in. God knows that many of us are no different from my then-adolescent sons. Our relationship with God, at least in the beginning, is need-based. Take away the need, and many, like the wealthy Laodiceans, would find little time to seek out God's will for their life.

Lukewarm is a dangerous state to be in. Those persons in such a state are often unaware that they are so precariously close to being considered a withered branch, separated from Jesus. This particular letter addresses those who are very comfortable with their lifestyle. Money, friends, and luxury occupy their hearts. Though they profess to be believers, there is no evidence of God being the center of their life. They are too busy enjoying their blessings to honor God with their life. Little do they know they are close to bankruptcy. They are described as pitiful, poor, blind and naked. Those living in this condition invest in the world instead of building treasures in Heaven.

Mathew 6:19-21 (NIV)
[19] *Do not store up for yourselves treasures on earth, where moths and vermin destroy, and where thieves break in and steal.*

20 But store up for yourselves treasures in heaven, where moths and vermin do not destroy, and where thieves do not break in and steal.
21 For where your treasure is, there your heart will be also.

Invest in the souls of people, the only commodity that will transfer from Earth to Heaven. People were deemed so precious that Jesus gave his life to save people.

Revelations 3:19-20 (NIV)
19 Those whom I love, I rebuke and discipline. So be earnest and repent.
20 Here I am! I stand at the door and knock. If anyone hears my voice and opens the door, I will come in and eat with that person, and they with me.

Oh, how He loves us! He rebukes and disciplines us because He loves us and does all He can to persuade us to turn from our ways that lead to destruction. Sometimes, He allows adverse circumstances to bring us to our knees. Very few people come to Christ when there is no hardship or perceptible void in their lives.

He stands at the door and knocks, but it is up to us to open the door.

Revelation 3:22 (NIV)
"He who has an ear, let him hear what the Spirit says to the churches."

Today's Promise

To the one who is victorious, I will give the right to sit with me on my throne, just as I was victorious and sat down with my Father on his throne.

Revelations 3:21

Bible Study Questions

Which of the three Churches discussed today resonated with you? Why?

_____

_____

_____

_____

_____

What action is required if any of the rebukes mentioned apply to you?

_____

_____

_____

_____

Notice that with every church (each of us), there is still an opportunity to correct. Which attributes of God stand out in these letters?

_____

_____

_____

_____

_____

Today's Prayer

Thank you, Lord, for allowing me to finish this study. Let the things I have learned and been reminded of take root in my heart so I can grow to have a stronger relationship with you. I want to hear you say, 'Good and Faithful servant, well done!' The only way I can finish this journey is with the help of your Spirit. Please fill me with Your Spirit to overflowing. I desire to please you and obey you in all of my ways. Forgive me when I fall short. Thank you for your strength in the areas I am weak. Hold Me close, never let me go!

You see Your people struggling in these wicked days. Help Your people to find truth and hold on to it - not to be deceived by false doctrine. Your people need an extension of grace and mercy. Thank you for being so patient and generous with us, your church.

Thoughts

_____

_____

_____

Group Questions

Has this study been helpful? If so, how?

What did you gain from the letters to us, the church?

Have you been encouraged in any way by this study? If so, how?

NOTES

176

Made in the USA
Middletown, DE
09 September 2024

60657842R00106